Cute Crochet World

A Little Dictionary of
Crochet Critters, Folks, Food & More

D1560872

Suzann Thompson

LARK

LARK

An Imprint of Sterling Publishing
387 Park Avenue South
New York, NY 10016

ISBN 978-1-4547-0806-3

Library of Congress Cataloging-in-Publication Data

Thompson, Suzann.
 Cute crochet world : a little dictionary of crochet critters, folks, food
& more / Suzann Thompson. -- First edition.
     pages cm
 Includes index.
 ISBN 978-1-4547-0806-3
 1. Crocheting--Patterns. I. Title.
 TT825.T488 2014
 746.43'4--dc23
                                           2013031612

Distributed in Canada by Sterling Publishing
c/o Canadian Manda Group, 165 Dufferin Street
Toronto, Ontario, Canada M6K 3H6
Distributed in the United Kingdom by GMC Distribution Services
Castle Place, 166 High Street, Lewes, East Sussex, England BN7 1XU
Distributed in Australia by Capricorn Link (Australia) Pty. Ltd.
P.O. Box 704, Windsor, NSW 2756, Australia

For information about custom editions, special sales, and premium and corporate purchases, please
contact Sterling Special Sales at 800-805-5489 or specialsales@sterlingpublishing.com.

Email academic@larkbooks.com for information about desk and examination copies.
The complete policy can be found at larkcrafts.com.

Manufactured in China

2 4 6 8 10 9 7 5 3 1

larkcrafts.com

contents

THE MOTIFS

introduction

Crocheters, I'm thrilled that you still enjoy making motifs for fun and embellishment!

We crocheters have gained a reputation for making fun things, but fun things can be practical, too. For instance, a fun Baby Carriage (page 106), appliquéd to a purchased fleece blanket, makes a very practical baby gift. Color-photocopy a fun Cozy Home (page 133) to create practical and beautiful house-warming party invitations. The sky's the limit!

For me, designing crocheted people, houses, and birds was a delightful and interesting challenge, especially after having written two books about crocheted flowers (*Crochet Bouquet* and *Crochet Garden*). I drew motifs over and over, trying to understand how they could be interpreted in crochet. The exercise expanded my thinking about how to make shapes and effects with crochet.

Inspiration for many of these projects came from daily life, but I often consulted illustrated children's books or Google images to find out things like: "Where exactly do a sea turtle's flippers attach to its body?" or "How long is a dachshund compared to how tall he is?"

The result of all this inspiration and experimentation is six chapters-worth of patterns for crocheting things from the everyday world and even from out of this world:

1. Land, sea, and, sky animals frolic, swim, and flutter through the "Critters" chapter.

2. In "Food," low-calorie treats include sweets, fruit, a yummy sandwich, and even a few vegetables.

3. You won't need a green thumb to raise the trees, mushrooms, and fruit in "Growing Things."

4. "Seasons" brings spring rains, summer skies, harvest moon, and gingerbread so cute you can almost smell it.

5. "Toys, Tools, Transportation" has you covered, from working in your garden to taking a very long trip.

6. Furnish and populate your crochet house inside and out with the motifs in "Home."

Two patterns use bullion stitch, which is new in my designing repertoire. I hope the trick described in "Read Me First" helps you make successful bullion stitches every time. You'll see a lot of slip stitch for outlining motifs, which makes edges look nice, minimizes curling, and allows you to add details on outer edges without having to cut and rejoin yarn too often. Another slip stitch variation is tambour stitching, used for adding detail within a motif.

You may be tempted to skip straight to the patterns, but please do read "Read Me First" first. The infamous "htr" is thoroughly explained, along with instructions for other stitches and techniques. In addition to information about supplies and tools, you'll find ideas for using the motifs in Cute Crochet World.

Why are there so many Martians in these pages? Many authors will tell you that characters in a book often take over and develop a life and style of their own. I think that's what happened here—and how lucky for us! Because remember when I told you that the sky's the limit? Well, if you crochet with green yarn and add antennae, the limit stretches to Mars—and beyond!

read me first!

SUPPLIES AND TOOLS

Yarn

Cute Crochet World lists the exact yarns used for each motif, and the resulting size of the motif. This is meant for your information, but not to limit you to any certain type of yarn. Since most of the motifs use small amounts of yarn, you can use yarns left over from other projects.

Your local yarn shop is the best place to find yarns, because you can touch the yarns and see their true colors. Maybe, like me, you don't have a local yarn shop. Time for a road trip! Or if that isn't in the cards, you can order yarn on the Internet.

Yarn and yarn colors go in and out of fashion, just like fabric, clothing, and cars. Within a couple of years after *Cute Crochet World* is published, most of the yarns used here will be discontinued. Think of this as an excuse to try new yarns.

I mostly used smooth yarns to make motifs, because you can see the shapes and details better. Go ahead and try other types of yarn—you may be pleasantly surprised how a novelty yarn affects the look of a motif.

If you use bulky yarn, your motif will be larger than the same motif crocheted in fine yarn. Look at the difference in size between the Oval Owls below. The larger one was made with Lion Brand's bulky Nature's Choice Organic Cotton. His little green friend, made from the very same pattern (except for the antennae), was crocheted with Aunt Lydia's Classic Crochet Thread No. 10.

YARN AMOUNTS

The motifs in *Cute Crochet World* require only a small amount of yarn. With one skein of each color listed for a motif,

you'll be able to crochet several or even many of the motif. Because of this, I list the colors only for each project, instead of repeating "one skein each of" over and over. If a pattern says "small amount of" a certain yarn, it usually means less than one yard (1 m).

Other Supplies

You may need:

- Polyester fiberfill: Use for stuffing three-dimensional motifs

- Beads: Use seed or bugle beads for eyes and other small details

- Embroidery floss: Use to create details on motifs

- Buttons, fabric glue, sewing thread, or other items as listed in individual pattern instructions

Hooks and Other Hardware

To make and finish the motifs in *Cute Crochet World*, you will need these tools:

- Crochet hooks in various sizes

- St markers: Use split ring style; also, paper clips, safety pins, even a short piece of contrasting yarn tied in a lp work as markers

- Tapestry needle: For weaving in yarn ends and sewing

- Scissors

- Other tools as listed in individual patterns, such as sewing or beading needles, or templates

Blocking Tools

Blocking your finished crochet pieces is commonly accepted best practice. Here's what you will need:

- Clean ironing surface, to which you can pin motifs if necessary

- Iron

- Clean, undyed press cloth

- Rust-proof straight pins

- Water

TECHNIQUES AND TIPS

Where to Find Basic Crochet Instructions

To make room for more patterns, we decided to leave beginning crochet instructions out of *Cute Crochet World*. If you don't know how to crochet yet, you can learn from the many excellent books, websites, and live teachers available to us today.

Contact your local yarn or craft shop to find out about beginning crochet classes, or ask if staff can direct you to a freelance teacher. Crochet guild members are usually eager to help beginners. In a class or guild, you'll pick up a new skill and probably make lifelong friendships at the same time.

For self-teaching, start at the Craft Yarn Council's website: www.craftyarncouncil.com. Follow the links to the crochet instruction pages and beyond.

Visit YouTube, where a group of dedicated crochet experts has created video tutorials of many crochet sts and techniques. Find them at www.youtube.com. Search for specific sts or the more general "crochet stitches."

My previous motif books, *Crochet Bouquet* and *Crochet Garden*, had no beginning crochet instructions either. This didn't stop determined beginners! Judith told me she learned how to crochet so she could crochet from my books. Andrea wrote, "These patterns make even a beginner feel accomplished and so happy!" Beginners, it can be done!

Gauge

Gauge refers to the tightness or looseness of your crochet sts. Loose sts make a project bigger and give it a softer hand. The same project crocheted tightly will be smaller and stiffer.

The motifs in this book require a firm gauge, which is not tight, but almost. The firm tension helps the motifs hold their shape. A firm gauge is neat and trim. It isn't floppy.

You'll know your tension is too tight if you have trouble inserting the hook into the sts. If your tension is too loose, the motifs will lose some of their definition, and some won't be able to hold up their own weight. A loosely crocheted motif will look less crisp.

The Craft Yarn Council's Standard Yarn Weight System chart (see chart on this page) lists a range of hooks that work best with different yarns. For a firm gauge, try the smallest hook in the range.

To test st tension, crocheters make a test swatch and measure sts and rows per inch

Standard Yarn Weight System

Yarn Weight Symbol & Category Names	(0) Lace	(1) Super Fine	(2) Fine	(3) Light	(4) Medium	(5) Bulky	(6) Super Bulky
Type of Yarns in Category	Fingering 10-count crochet thread	Sock, Fingering, Baby	Sport, Baby	DK, Light Worsted	Worsted, Afghan, Aran	Chunky, Craft, Rug	Bulky, Roving
Crochet Gauge Ranges in Single Crochet to 4 inch	32-42 double crochets	21-32 sts	16-20 sts	12-17 sts	11-14 sts	8-11 sts	5-9 sts
Recommended Hook in Metric Size Range	Steel 2.25-1.4 mm	2.25-3.5 mm	3.5-4.5 mm	4.5-5.5 mm	5.5-6.5 mm	6.5-9 mm	9 mm and larger
Recommended Hook U.S. Size Range	Steel 3, 4, 5, 6, 7, 8 Regular hook B-1	B-1 to E-4	E-4 to 7	7 to I-9	I-9 to K-10½	K-10½ to M-13	M-13 and larger

Note: The recommended hook sizes in this chart reflect those used for the projects only in this book.

before embarking on a new project. (You do, right?) A traditional 4" x 4" (10 x 10 cm) gauge swatch would probably take you longer to make than almost any motif in *Cute Crochet World*. Frankly, with such small motifs, st tension doesn't have the same effect that it does in a larger project, such as a sweater. So how can we test st tension without crocheting a (relatively) large gauge swatch? The answer is gauge circles. Here's how to make one:

Ch 4, join with a sl st in first ch to form a ring.

Rnd 1: ch 2, 11 hdc in ring, cut thread and needle-join to first st of rnd.

To measure the gauge circle, place it *on top* of a measuring tape or ruler. Arrange it so the inch or cm mark barely shows at one edge of it. Note which mark shows at

Gauge circles are quicker than traditional gauge swatches. To measure your gauge circle, put it on top of the measuring tape.

the opposite edge of the piece, remove the gauge circle, and determine how wide it is (its diameter).

If your gauge circle is larger than mine, you might want to use a smaller hook; if it is smaller, try a larger hook.

Good things about the gauge circle: You will have lots of practice with needle-joining, you can use gauge circles for appliqué details, and you can use them for fillers in Crochet Charm Lace (page 14).

From shortest on the right to tallest on the left, we have: sl st, sc, hdc, dc, htr, tr, hdtr, dtr. Note the smooth incline made possible by the half-sts.

Htr Means Half-Treble

The half-treble, or htr, is a step in height between the double crochet (dc) and the treble crochet (tr). When a dc is too short and a tr is too tall, the htr is perfect!

I wish I had invented the htr, but no, the incomparable Thérèse de Dillmont described it in her book, *The Complete Encyclopedia of Needlework*, written in 1884. She went on to propose half-sts between even taller crochet sts.

In UK crochet terminology, htr = hdtr.

Here's how to make an htr:

Yo (twice). Insert hook in next st and draw up a lp (4 lps on hook).

Yo and draw through 2 lps on hook (3 lps on hook).

Yo and draw through rem lps on hook (1 lp on hook).

Front Loop and Back Loop

Unless instructed otherwise, catch the top two lps of any crochet st as you work. Sometimes a pattern directs you to crochet in the front lp only or back lp only (abbreviated FLO and BLO). The front lp is the one that is closest to you as you work, regardless of whether you're working in the

Create a look of corrugated cupcake paper, found on the Cupcake on page 54, by crocheting in the BL of every row of sc.

round or back and forth. The back lp is the one that is away from you as you work.

The FL is the lp that is closest to you *at the moment you are crocheting into the st.* Same with the BL. Live in the present.

First Stitch and Next Stitch

At the beginning of a row or round, we make a turning ch of one or more ch-sts to bring the hook up to the level of the st to be used in the row. For taller sts, like hdc, dc, and so on, the turning chain acts as the first st.

For instance, when you ch 3 at the start of a row of dc-sts, it counts as the first dc. In these patterns, you'll see "(counts as dc)" for the first row or so, to remind you to count it as a st. Since it counts as the first st, you normally sk the first st (which is the last st of the previous row). That is why the instructions tell you to work into the "next st."

However, sometimes you need to increase at the edge, and then the instructions will tell you to put a st into the "first st."

In this dc sample, the ch-3 at the start of each row counts as one dc. It is the st in the "first" st of the row below (A). The first actual dc you crochet will be in the "next" st (B). Also, don't forget to dc into the turning ch of the previous row when you come to the end of the row you're working on (C).

WHICH ONE IS THE NEXT STITCH?

This may seem like a silly question, but sometimes it's hard to tell which st really is next. Here are some hints:

- Sometimes you make a st, and it slides back and tricks you into thinking that it is in the previous st. You happily put another st into the same place and wonder why your count is off at the end of the row. If in doubt, pull your last st up gently. If the "next st" pulls along with your st, it isn't the next st. Move on to the *real* next st.

- When you have just made lots of sts into a ch-sp, they often cover the top of the "next st." Pull them back, out of the way, to find the next st.

- At the beginning of a row of hdc, dc, htr, or tr, the turning ch is coming out of the first st, and the "next st" is the second st.

- At the beginning of a round, after a sl-st join, you'll often find that the "next st" has been distorted by the sl-st join. Be aware of this as you work the next round. Counting sts will help.

With experience, you will consider all these things automatically as you crochet. It's well worth the time to pay attention to these picky details.

Decreasing

To decrease in crochet, begin two (or more) sts, but stop short of the last yo/pull-through, which would normally finish the st. When you have begun all the sts you want to decrease, only then do you yo and pull through all the unfinished lps. On the next row or round, you will see one st, where there were two (or more).

A more specific example is "dc2tog," which means "double crochet 2 sts together." Here's how:

Yo, draw up a lp in next st (3 lps on hook).

Yo, pull through 2 lps on hook (2 lps on hook). *Now the first dc is begun, but stopped just short of the final yo/pull-through.*

Yo, draw up a lp in next st (4 lps on hook).

Yo, pull through 2 lps on hook (3 lps on hook). *The second dc is begun and stopped just short of its final yo/pull-through.*

To finish the dc2tog, yo and pull through all 3 lps on hook.

Some patterns require you to decrease two different-size sts, like "dc-hdc-tog." This means "decrease by crocheting a dc and an hdc together." It operates on the same basic principle:

Yo, draw up a lp in next st (3 lps on hook).

Yo, pull through 2 lps on hook (2 lps on hook). *Now the dc is begun, but stopped just short of the final yo/pull-through.*

Yo, draw up a lp in next st (5 lps on hook). *The hdc is begun, but stopped before the last yo/pull-through.*

To finish the dc-hdc-tog, yo and pull through all 5 lps on hook.

Working in the Free Loops of the Foundation Chain

When you have worked a row of sts into the foundation ch, and then you rotate the work and crochet into the ch again, you are working into what I call the free lps of the foundation ch. You are working in the ch-sts on the opposite side of the foundation ch. It's a technique used for shaping crochet. In this book, instructions alert you when you will be working into the free lps of a foundation ch (or the opposite side of the foundation ch), then tell you which st or sts to work into successive ch-sts.

"Rotate" is different from "turn." When you rotate, you are still looking at the same side of the work. To turn means that you flip the work to the other side.

Row 1 of the Bluebird of Happiness (page 24) is complete, and I have made the first 3 hdc of Row 2. To complete Row 2, I will have to make hdc in the next 5 free lps or ch-sts of the foundation ch. Can you see which lps I will be working into?

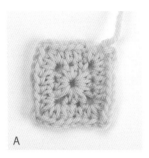

A

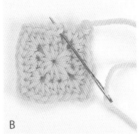

B

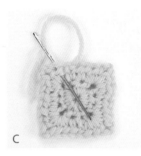

C

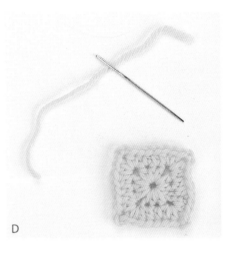

D

Needle–Join

For a seamless-looking finish, join rounds of crochet with the needle-join. I almost always join rounds with needle-join because it looks good and it eliminates the irritating knot formed by a sl-st join.

Here's how to do the needle-join:

Complete last st of round.

With hook still in last lp, cut yarn, leaving an end about 4"/10cm long.

Pull hook straight up from st, so yarn end will come out of top of st. (Photo A shows yarn end pulled through.)

Thread yarn into a tapestry needle.

Look at top of first st of round. This may be a ch-2 (acting as first hdc, as in the sample above) or ch-3 (acting as first dc)—if so, then last ch is top of st.

Following yarn lp at top of first st, insert your needle from front to back, under lps of second st (Photo B).

Insert needle into top of last st, catching back lp and yarn lp under that. (Photo C shows sample from back.)

Yarn comes out at back of work. Tighten new lp to match lps at top of other sts.

Original top of first st may add extra bulk at this join. Push or pull it to the back, and weave yarn end through it to keep it at the back.

The finished join doesn't look like a join at all (Photo D).

By replacing the top lp of the first st with a needle-join, you will preserve the correct number of sts in the round.

Needle-join looks especially nice when used to join a sl-st outline. Look at the outline around the Kiwi below. You can't tell where it begins and ends. When you're needle-joining a sl-st round, stop one st short of the end, cut yarn and pull out as in A above. In step B, skim needle under the threads of the first st of the round, take needle back into the last st, to the back, and weave in end.

A needle-join can be for looks only, like when you join the stem of a leaf to its base, as in the Horse Chestnut Leaf at left. Certainly you could join with a sl st. This makes an unsightly bump, which I don't like, so I think that a needle-join is well worth the time for a better finish.

Kite with tambour st in progress. Note how the working thread is underneath the Kite, but the sts are on the top surface.

This shows what a bullion st in progress looks like after step 4. The hook and needle are wrapped, a lp has been drawn up in ring, and this drawn-up lp is underneath the tapestry needle.

The finished bullion st practice piece.

Tambour Stitch

Traditional tambour is a chained embroidery st, formed with a small hook instead of a needle. The top of the chain creates the design on top of the fabric. The wrong side of the chain, or the bump of the chain, is on the underside of the wrong side of the fabric.

Crocheters use tambour st to add detail or an outline, as in the Kite above. It is like making sl sts through the middle of a motif. In general, you work one tambour st for each crochet st across a row of sts: one tambour st to cover the depth of one sc st. Sometimes you must use your judgment about where you will insert the hook, and how tight or loose the st tension should be.

To make tambour st, hold the motif with the right side toward you. Hold the yarn under the motif. *Insert hook from right side to wrong side, yo, pull a lp through to right side of motif; rep from * as directed.

To finish a line of tambour sts, cut yarn and pull last yo to front of work until the yarn end comes through. Thread yarn end into tapestry needle. Take yarn back through the motif to the wrong side, so that it catches the last full lp and keeps it from unraveling. Weave in end.

Bullion Stitch

Another crochet technique inspired by embroidery, the bullion st features many wraps that are held in place by a drawn-up lp and a ch-st. Bullion st adds rich texture to crochet.

Basically, you wrap yarn around the crochet hook anywhere from 4 to 20 times, draw up a lp in the piece you are working on, letting the yarn flow freely, draw the same lp through all wraps on the hook, and ch 1 to lock in the wraps. A strand of yarn runs up the side. Avoid pulling the yarn (unless instructions tell you to), so the bullion st can stand up straight.

As you might guess, this is easier said than done. I found a wonderful trick on YouTube that helps me make good bullion sts most of the time. Let's make a practice piece to learn this technique. You'll need a tapestry needle.

BULLION PRACTICE PIECE
Ch 5, join with sl st to first ch to form lp, ch 5 as a turning ch. To make each bullion st:

1. Hold a tapestry needle in line with your hook, with the eye covering the hook end. The needle should go under the lp on your hook.

2. Wrap yarn around hook and tapestry needle 12 times, carefully laying each wrap next to the previous wrap, and keeping the needle in line with your hook.

3. Holding wraps in place, slide the tapestry needle back just slightly so the hook is free.

4. Still holding wraps in place, insert hook into ring and draw up a lp.

5. Slide the tapestry needle back over hooked end to lock the pulled-up lp underneath.

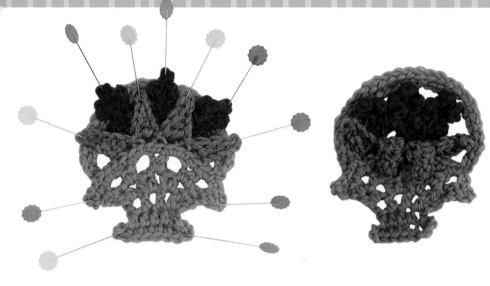

Here's how I pinned out the Flower Basket (far left) for blocking. The unblocked Flower Basket is for comparison. (This project can be found on page 70.)

6. Keeping the needle aligned over the hooked part of the hook, use your yarn-holding thumb and index finger to hold the lps.

7. Slide hook through the lps, making sure you keep the hook itself centered along the needle, and pull enough thread through to allow room for all the wraps to sit without overlapping. Remove the tapestry needle from the wraps if it doesn't come out on its own.

8. The yarn will come out from the base of the bullion st. Your hook is at the top of the st. Ch 1 to lock the st, making sure the thread is plenty long, running up the side of the st, so the st will stand straight as possible.

9. Repeat the steps for the bullion st until the ring is full of sts. Sl st in top of first bullion st of ring. Fasten off.

Practice will make you more comfortable with this method. You'll soon be ready to make Vintage Grapes (page 67) and a Valentine Roses (page 92).

Blocking and Finishing

Unless the yarn label advertises "no blocking required," blocking is commonly accepted best practice for finishing crochet projects.

Wool, mohair, linen, and cotton respond well to steam blocking. Blends of these natural fibers with synthetics do fine with steam blocking as well. I am more comfortable using the cool, wet-blocking method with silk, silk blends, and synthetic fibers. If in doubt, block a small sample to see how it responds.

COOL, WET BLOCKING

Douse the motif with water.

Squeeze out as much water as you can. You may roll the motif in a towel and press out more water, but DO NOT WRING.

Spread the motif on your blocking surface.

Unfurl and stretch out points, petals, leaves.

For best results, pin the points of leaves and petals, especially if they curl stubbornly (see photo of Flower Basket above).

Let dry.

STEAM BLOCKING

Heat the iron (you can use steam or not).

Wet a press cloth, and wring out the excess water.

Spread the motif on the blocking surface.

Unfurl and stretch out points, petals, leaves.

Pin points of leaves or petals for best results.

Lay the press cloth over the motif.

Touch the hot iron to the press cloth, letting your hand hold the weight of the iron.

The steam will go into the motif.

Remove the press cloth and make sure the motif looks the way you want it. Readjust pins if desired.

Let cool and dry.

USING THESE MOTIFS

What can you do with these projects from *Cute Crochet World*? Here are a few ideas. You'll undoubtedly come up with more.

Decorate

Use motifs to decorate clothing, fashion accessories, or home accessories.

Appliqué flat motifs by sewing around outer edges, then tacking in a few places in the body of the motif to keep it from sagging.

If you prefer to glue, squeeze fabric glue onto a folded piece of paper and use a short-bristle brush to paint glue onto the wrong side of motif. Once the motif is glued in place, weight it with a flat object like a book. Leave plenty of time for the glue to dry.

My personal favorite appliqué method is to glue AND sew around the outside of a motif.

Give Motifs to Children

My fourth-grade daughter carried motifs in the see-through pocket on the outside of her ring binder. She loved to show them off. One day when a friend was feeling sad, she gave her friend a motif to cheer her up. Motifs can fall out of notebook cover pockets, so tape the opening shut.

Young children will love to play with three-dimensional food items in particular (avoid giving them items decorated with beads). They will happily "bake" you pie and make you a sandwich, as long as you are willing to play along. You can also teach: "Oh look, this green pie must be a gooseberry pie! What flavor do you think this blue pie is?" or "Could this be Cheddar cheese?" or "You must have brushed this pie crust with egg to get that lovely golden color!"

Make Jewelry or Ornaments

Sew a pin finding to the back of a three-dimensional motif to make a brooch.

To make a simple necklace:

1. Make a chain of ch-st, at least 10"/26cm long.

2. Sl st into the top of the motif.

3. Continue ch-st to match the length of the first chain (at least 10"/26cm long) PLUS 2 sts, turn.

4. Sc in 2nd ch from hook, sl st in each ch, stopping 1 st short of the sl st that attaches the chain to the motif.

5. Sk the ch before the sl st, sk the sl st, sk the ch after the sl st.

6. Sl st in each ch, until 1 ch remains. Sc in last ch. Fasten off.

7. Weave in ends. Tie the necklace around your neck and enjoy!

Add a crocheted or ribbon hanging lp to a motif and use it as an ornament.

To use flat motifs for jewelry or ornaments, first stabilize by gluing or sewing the motif to a piece of felt. Lay the motif face-up on the felt and outline with a pen. Cut out the shape from the felt, then sew or glue the felt to the wrong side of the motif. Add jewelry findings or a hanging lp.

Additional tips for using the motifs can be found in many of the projects!

Tell a Story

Group motifs and sew to a table runner or wall hanging to tell a story. For instance, show the story of your family using Cozy Home (page 133); Cherry Blossom (page 76); parents (Mamas and Papas, page 137); children (Costumed Kids, page 128, or Baby Carriage, page 106); and pets (Weiner Dog, page 40).

You'll find motifs here to tell lots of stories: maybe about your summer vacation, or a tall tale about persons from outer space.

Make Custom Stationery

Photograph or scan motifs that you have crocheted and use the digital images to create custom stationery, invitations, or thank-you notes. If you don't have a color printer, take your digital files to a printer or office supply store with a printing department. They can print your images on all kinds of things, from fancy cardstock to posters.

By using digital images, you can resize motifs to make your pictures more realistic (or less realistic, if you want).

Or you can make greeting cards the old-fashioned way: make motifs with fine yarn or thread, and then glue them to blank cards (available at craft supply stores).

Create Crochet Charm Lace

Crochet Charm Lace is made from crocheted motifs, which are sewn together in any shape. The effect is lacy. For step-by-step photos of Crochet Charm Lace using flower motifs, please visit Lark Crafts's blog: www.larkcrafts.com/needlearts/trillium-flower-cloth-scarf-project-from-suzann-thompson.

First decide what you want to make. It can be anything you can cut from fabric, and probably more. To familiarize yourself with the technique, begin with a flat project, like a scarf, table runner, or doily.

Cut the shape of your project from a piece of sturdy fabric. The fabric won't be part of the finished project.

I traced around a dinner plate to create the template for this doily, made with Summer Sun and Bluebird of Happiness motifs, and Gauge Circles (page 7) for fillers. I safety pinned the motifs, face-down, on the fabric template and sewed them together wherever they touched.

The safety pins and fabric template are gone, and the doily is turned face-up. The first look at the finished work is thrilling!

Gather yarns of any size, texture, and fiber content. I usually try to unify my yarn choices by picking yarns in one color family or sticking to a few colors. Or you can use all the same type of yarn—whatever you want, because gauge doesn't matter.

Crochet enough motifs to cover your fabric, plus a few. Make some small motifs, like gauge circles (page 7) or motifs in light weight yarns. Weave in all the ends and block the motifs.

Arrange the motifs face-down on the fabric, with their edges touching wherever possible. Whenever you have a gap that is just too large for your liking, but too small for a regular motif, use a gauge circle or tiny motif to fill in.

Safety pin the motifs in place.

Use sewing thread, embroidery floss, or fine yarn to sew the edges of the motifs together. Since the motifs are face-down, the sewing sts will be on the wrong side of the work. Keep the sts small. You will need to tack and cut thread fairly often. Avoid sewing through the safety pins.

Remove the pins and fabric. Turn your piece right side up. Admire your finished work!

CONTACT ME

If you need help with any pattern in this book, please contact me, Suzann Thompson, the author. At Ravelry (www.ravelry.com), an online knitting and crochet community that is free to join, my tag is "textilefusion." You can send me a message there.

Check out my book blog, "Curious and Crafty Readers," where you'll find Crochet-Alongs with patterns from *Cute Crochet World*, as well as tutorials (especially if you ask for them), ideas for using these crocheted motifs, and more. Please leave a comment at the blog, or contact me by email. Find a link to my email address at the blog site, www.textilefusion.com/bookblog.

I also have an author page on Facebook, where I post book news.

Please send me your comments and suggestions, too. I will be very glad to hear from you.

abbreviations and definitions

Crochet Stitch Abbreviations

2dc-cluster: [Yo, draw up lp in indicated st, yo and draw through 2 lps on hook] twice (3 lps on hook). Yo and draw through all lps on hook to complete cluster.

BL: Back lp

BLO: Back lp only

BP (back post): This tells you to work around the body (or post) of a st, instead of working into the top. Insert hook from back of your work to front on the near side of the st, and to the back again on the far side of the st. The st will appear behind, or in BACK, of your hook. The top of the st, which you would normally crochet into (but not this time), is pushed toward you. To remember this I visualize my hook in the BACK before it goes around the POST (back post).

> **BPdc (back post double crochet):** Work a dc around the post of the indicated st, as described above under BP.

> **BPhdc (back post half double crochet):** Work an hdc around the post of the indicated st, as described above under BP.

> **BPsc (back post single crochet):** Work an sc around the post of the indicated st, as described above under BP.

Dc (double crochet): Yo, draw up lp in indicated st (3 lps on hook), [yo and draw through 2 lps on hook] twice.

Dc2tog: [Yo, draw up lp in next st, yo, pull through 2 lps on hook] twice. Now you have 3 lps on hook. Yo and pull through all lps on hook.

Dc3tog: [Yo, draw up lp in indicated st, yo, pull through 2 lps on hook] 3 times. Now you have 4 lps on hook. Yo and pull through all lps on hook.

Dc-hdc-sctog: Yo, draw up lp in indicated st, yo, pull through 2 lps (for dc), yo, draw up lp in indicated st (for hdc), draw up lp in indicated st (for sc), yo and draw through all lps on hook.

Draw up lp: Insert hook in st, yo, pull yarn through the st only. Sometimes the yarn is attached to a previous st; if not, be sure to leave a yarn end long enough to prevent the st from coming out.

FL: Front lp

FLO: Front lp only

FP (front post): This tells you to work around the body (or post) of a st, instead of working into the top. Insert hook from the front of your work to back on the near side of the st, and to the front again on the far side of the st. The st will be in FRONT of your hook. The top of the st, which you would normally crochet into (but not this time), is pushed away from you. To remember this I visualize my hook in the FRONT before it goes around the POST (front post).

> **FPdc (front post double crochet):** Work a dc around the post of the indicated st, as described above under FP.

> **FPhdc (front post half double crochet):** Work an hdc around the post of the indicated st, as described above under FP.

> **FPsc (front post single crochet):** Work an sc around the post of the indicated st, as described above under FP.

Free lp: A free lp is at the base of a st that has been worked into a ch. It is the lp of the ch left over after you st into the ch. (See page 9.)

Hdc: Yo, draw up lp in indicated st (3 lps on hook), yo and draw through all lps on hook.

Hdc2tog: [Yo, draw up lp in next st on hook] twice. Now you have 5 lps on hook. Yo and pull through all lps on hook.

Htr (half-treble): Yo (twice), draw up lp (4 lps on hook), yo and draw through 2 lps on hook (3 lps on hook), yo and draw through remaining 3 lps on hook.

Htr2tog: [Yo (twice), draw up lp in next st, yo, draw through 2 lps on hook] twice (5 lps on hook), yo and draw through all lps on hook.

Join with dc: With a slip knot on hook, yo and draw up lp in indicated st (3 lps on hook), [yo and draw through 2 lps on hook] twice. You may have to hold onto the original knot to keep the yo from disappearing before its time.

Join with hdc: With a slip knot on hook, yo and draw up lp in indicated st (3 lps on hook), yo and draw through all lps on hook. You may have to hold onto the original knot to keep the yo from disappearing before its time.

Join with sc: With a slip knot on hook, draw up lp in indicated st (2 lps on hook), yo and draw through all lps on hook.

Join with tr: With a slip knot on hook, Yo (twice) and draw up lp in indicated st (4 lps on hook), [yo and draw through 2 lps on hook] three times. You may have to hold onto the original knot to keep the yos from disappearing before their time.

Joined-dc (st is worked next to a ch-3, which takes the place of a dc at the beginning of a row): Yo, draw up lp in 2nd ch from hook, draw up lp in next st (3 lps on hook), [yo, draw through 2 lps on hook]

twice to finish dc. This keeps the ch-3 from creating a gap.

Joined-tr (st is worked next to ch-4 at the beginning of a row): Yo, draw up lp in 3rd ch from hook, draw up lp in next st (4 lps on hook), [yo, draw through 2 lps on hook] 3 times to finish tr. This keeps the ch-4 from creating a gap.

Lp: Loop

PM: Place marker

Rem: Remain(ing)

Rep: Repeat

RM: Remove marker

RS: Right side of work

Sc: Draw up lp in indicated st (2 lps on hook), yo and draw through all lps on hook.

Sc2tog: Draw up lp in each of next 2 sts, yo and draw through all lps on hook.

Sc-picot (single crochet picot): Ch 3, sc in 3rd ch from hook.

Sk: Skip

Sl st (slip stitch): Insert hook in indicated st, yo and draw through all lps on hook.

Slst-picot (slip stitch picot): Ch 3, sl st in 3rd ch from hook. If the instructions tell

you to "ch 7, slst-picot," then you should work ch 7, then ch 3 more, sl st in 3rd ch from hook.

St-top-picot (stitch-top picot): Ch 3, insert hook in FL of st before ch-sts, insert hook under the lp immediately under the FL of the st (it will lie at a slight angle to the FL of the st), yo and draw through all lps on hook. This picot minimizes the space between the sts on either side of it.

Tambour st: See page 11. This is a sl st used for outline—work it into sts or sides of sts. Sometimes worked across a piece, where you hold the yarn on the wrong side of work and insert hook through work from RS to WS, yo, and pull through.

Tr (treble crochet): Yo (twice), draw up lp in indicated st (4 lps on hook), [yo, draw through 2 lps on hook] 3 times.

Tr2tog: *Yo (twice), draw up lp in next st, [yo, draw through 2 lps on hook] twice; rep from * once (3 lps on hook), yo and draw through all lps on hook.

Tr-dctog: Yo (twice), draw up lp in next st, [yo, draw through 2 lps on hook] twice, yo, draw up lp in next st, yo and draw through 2 lps on hook (3 lps on hook), yo and draw through all lps on hook.

WS: Wrong side of work

U.S. and UK Crochet Stitches

Cute Crochet World was written using abbreviations of U.S. crochet terms. This chart gives the UK equivalents:

U.S. Crochet Abbreviation	UK Crochet Abbreviation
Sc	Dc
Hdc	Htr
Dc	Tr
Htr (see instructions on page 16)	Hdtr (see instructions for htr on page 16)
Trc	Dtr
3dc-cluster	3tr-cluster
BPdc	BPtr

Pattern Reading Tips

Parentheses ( ) are intended to group sts. For instance, "(hdc, sc) in the next st" alerts you to the fact that there is an hdc and an sc together and you need to read further to find out how they will be used.

Brackets [ ] group stitches for repetition: [dc2tog over next 2 sts, dc in next st] 3 times = dc2tog over next 2 sts, dc in next st, dc2tog over next 2 sts, dc in next st, dc2tog over next 2 sts, dc in next st.

Single asterisks * and double asterisks ** are markers in the pattern. Ignore them until the instructions refer to them. Most of the time, you'll see instructions such as "Repeat from * 3 times." You have already followed the instructions once. Now repeat them 3 times. When you're finished, you will have followed the instructions 4 times in all.

When instructions seem overwhelming, try making a flip book: Copy each row or round of a pattern onto a separate index card, punch a hole in one corner of each card, then bind with a binder loop or tie them together with a piece of yarn. Having the rows on separate cards stops your eye from accidentally "finding your place" in the wrong row. You will be amazed at how much better you understand the pattern after you write it out.

Also, read instructions aloud to yourself. Sometimes hearing the instructions clarifies them in your mind. You may want to ask someone to read the instructions aloud to you as you crochet. Reading a pattern aloud takes some skill, because the reader has to know how to pace the reading, and how much to read so the crocheter can make sense of it all. You'll both need some patience to make this work.

Look for hints to orient yourself in the pattern. In writing these patterns, I often used the abbreviations RS (right side) and WS (wrong side) to help you position your crocheting correctly. If you have trouble keeping up with the RS and WS of a piece, place a safety pin on the RS as indicated in the pattern, as a visual aid.

Use the st counts provided at the end of most rows or rounds to help you figure out whether you have crocheted the row correctly. Remember to count turning-chains of 2 or more as sts.

the motifs

As you turn this page, imagine that you are opening the door to a world populated with happy families and their quaint houses and cute pets. They enjoy being out in nature, even when the weather is windy or wet. They cook tasty treats. They make music or relax in front of the television. Enter their world and find something to make that will delight you and the people you love.

ladybug, ladybug

Children of all ages love the pretty ladybug. But she (or he) is also a fearless protector of our spring gardens. Aphids: Don't even think about settling on our plants!

SKILL LEVEL
Intermediate

MATERIALS & TOOLS
Yarn: Red (A), black (B)

Crochet hook: Appropriate size hook to achieve a firm gauge with selected yarn

Small amount of polyester fiberfill stuffing

Tapestry needle

PATTERN NOTE
Read about tambour st on page 11.

ABBREVIATIONS
Find instructions on page 17 for: PM.

Ladybug leg: Ch 4, sl st in 3rd ch from hook, sl st in next ch.

FOR THESE LADYBUGS WE USED
Dale of Norway Falk (100% superwash wool; 1¾oz/50g = 116yd/106m) DK weight yarn (3): #4018 Red, #3609 Poppy, or #8817 Lime (A), #0090 Black (B).

GAUGE CIRCLE
(see page 7) = 1"/2.5cm worked on 4.00mm (size G-6 U.S.) hook

FINISHED MEASUREMENT
1¾"/4.5cm wide x 2⅛"/5.5cm long

INSTRUCTIONS

TOP

With A, ch 4, join with sl st to form a ring.

Rnd 1: Ch 1, 6 sc in ring, join with sl st to first sc. (6 sc)

Rnd 2: Ch 1, 2 sc in each st around, join with sl st to first sc. (12 sc)

Rnd 3: Ch 2 (counts as hdc), hdc in next st, pull last lp out large, so it won't come undone as you work the next section of Rnd 3. Attach B with 2 sc in next st, ch 2, sk next st, 2 sc in next st, ch 4, sk next 3 sts, 2 sc in next st, ch 2, sk next st, 2 sc in next st, ch 1. Fasten off B.

Insert hook into last lp of A and tighten lp. Continuing with A, *sc in each of next 2 B-color sc-sts, fold the B ch-sp out of the way toward the back of the work, 2 hdc in next st of Rnd 2, sc in each of next 2 B-color sc-sts*; fold the ch-4 lp of B out of the way toward the back of the work, hdc in each of next 3 sts of Rnd 2, rep bet * to * once, hdc in next st of Rnd 2, join with sl st to top of ch-2 at beg of rnd. (18 sts in color A)

Rnd 4: Ch 1, sc in each of first 10 sts, PM in last st, sc in each of next 8 sts, join with sl st to first st of rnd. Fasten off, leaving a long sewing length. (18 sc)

Place a lp of B onto hook, insert hook into the marked st of Rnd 4. Holding thread underneath the ladybug top, work 9-10 tambour sts across the ladybug top, keeping them centered between the pairs of spots.

Ladybug head

With B, ch 2, draw up a lp in the st that is before the tambour line (to the right for most crocheters), draw lp through st on hook, ch 1, sc in same st as drawn-up-lp (you will probably end up stitching over the ch-2, and this is fine), sc in the st where the tambour line ends, 2 sc in next st. Fasten off, leaving a long sewing length.

UNDERSIDE

With B, ch 4, join with sl st to form a ring.

Rnd 1: Ch 1, 8 sc in ring, join with sl st to first st of rnd. (8 sc)

Rnd 2: Ch 1, 2 sc in each st around, join with sl st to first sc. (16 sc)

Rnd 3: Ch 1, sc in next 2 sts, 2 sc in next st, make a ladybug leg (see Abbreviations at left), (sc, make a ladybug leg, sc) in next st, sc in next st, make a ladybug leg, [2 sc in next st, sc in next st] 3 times, make a ladybug leg, sc in next st, (sc, make a ladybug leg, sc) in next st, make a ladybug leg, sc in next st, 2 sc in next st.

Ladybug head

Ch 1, 2 hdc in next st, sc in first sc of Rnd 3, 2 sc in next sc. Fasten off.

FINISHING

Place ladybug top onto ladybug underside, lining up the heads. Use the long A sewing length to sew the top to the bottom, stuffing with the yarn ends and some polyester fiberfill if needed. Use the long B sewing length to sew the head sections together. Weave in ends.

For Even More Fun...

Attach a safety pin to the back of your ladybug and, presto! You have a super-cute brooch to pin to coats, hats, or shirts.

chicks

Downy baby chicks learn fast: how to scratch and peck for food, how to call their mama hen with high, sweet peeps, and how to hide under mama's feathers when they are frightened or sleepy.

SKILL LEVEL
Intermediate

MATERIALS & TOOLS
2 colors of yarn: Chick color (A), leg color (B)

Crochet hook: Appropriate size hook to achieve a firm gauge with selected yarn

Tapestry needle

ABBREVIATIONS
Find instructions on page 17 for: slst-picot

For Even More Fun...
How adorable would a set of three of these chicks look on a baby's onesie?

INSTRUCTIONS

RIGHT-FACING CHICK BODY

With A, ch 5, join with sl st to form a ring.

Rnd 1: Ch 3 (counts as dc), (5 dc, hdc, 2 sc, hdc, 5 dc) in ring, join with sl st to top of ch-3 at beg of rnd.

Rnd 2: Ch 3, 2 dc in next dc, dc in next dc, 2 dc in each of next 2 dc, (2 dc, hdc, sc) in next dc, sc in next 4 sts, (sc, hdc, slst-picot, dc, slst-picot, dc, slst-picot, ch 2, sc) in next dc, hdc in next dc, 2 dc in each of next 3 dc, join with sl st to top of ch-3 at beg of rnd, OR for lovelier results, cut yarn and needle-join to beg of rnd.

LEFT-FACING CHICK BODY

Using A, ch 5, join with sl st to form a ring.

Rnd 1: Ch 3 (counts as 1 dc), (5 dc, hdc, 2 sc, hdc, 5 dc) in ring, join with sl st to top of ch-3 at beg of rnd.

FOR THESE CHICKS WE USED

Dale of Norway Falk (100% superwash wool; 1¾oz/50g = 116yd/106m) DK weight yarn (3): #2417 yellow (A), #3309 orange (B).

> **GAUGE CIRCLE**
> (see page 7) = 1"/2.5cm worked
> on 4.00mm (size G-6 U.S.) hook
>
> **FINISHED MEASUREMENT**
> Body and head only 3"/7.5cm x 2"/5cm

Ivy Brambles SockScene (100% superwash merino; 4oz/113g = 410yd/378m) superfine yarn (1): #106 Buttercup (A), #108 Day Glow (B).

> **GAUGE CIRCLE**
> (see page 7) = ¾"/2cm worked
> on 3.25mm (size 0 steel U.S.) hook
>
> **FINISHED MEASUREMENT**
> Body and head only 2½"/6.5cm x
> 1⅜"/3.5cm

Lion Brand Kitchen Cotton (100% cotton; 2oz/57g = 99yd/90m) medium weight yarn (4): #157 Citrus (A), #133 Pumpkin (B).

> **GAUGE CIRCLE**
> (see page 7) = 1¼"/3cm worked
> on 5.00mm (size H-8 U.S.) hook
>
> **FINISHED MEASUREMENT**
> Body and head only 4½"/11.5cm x
> 2½"/6.5cm

Rnd 2: Ch 3, 2 dc in each of next 3 dc, hdc in next dc, (sc, ch 2, slst-picot, dc, slst-picot, dc, slst-picot, hdc, sc) in next st, sc in next 4 sts, (sc, hdc, 2dc) in next st, 2 dc in each of next 2 dc, dc in next dc, 2 dc in next dc, join with sl st to top of ch-3 at beg of rnd, OR for lovelier results, cut yarn and needle-join to beg of rnd.

CHICK HEAD

Using A, ch 4, join with sl st to form a ring.

Rnd 1: Ch 3, 4 dc in ring.

To form beak, (ch 3, sl st in 2nd ch from hook, sl st in next ch) twice, sl st into first ch of beak. Continuing with head, 7 dc in original ring. Leaving a long sewing length, fasten off or cut yarn and needle-join.

CHICK LEGS

Position legs as desired for a running chick (one leg closer to tail, one leg closer to head), standing chick (both legs centered between head and tail), chick calling its mama (both legs closer to tail), or eating chick (both legs closer to head).

For each leg, join B with sl st in desired st of chick's belly, ch 3, [ch 3, sl st in 2nd ch from hook, sl st in next ch] 3 times, sl st in next 3 ch-sts, sl st into same st of the bird's belly where the first st is attached. Fasten off B.

FINISHING

With sewing length, sew head to body using photos as a guide for placement. A running, eating, or calling chick's head is at the very tip of the body opposite the tail. A standing chick's head slightly overlaps the point of the body. Weave in ends.

bluebird of happiness

These are busy birds! You choose whether they sing, fly, or walk around by crocheting different beak styles, wings, or feet.

FOR THESE BIRDS WE USED

Coats & Clark Aunt Lydia's Classic Crochet Thread, No. 10, Art. 154 (100% mercerized cotton; 350yd/320m) 10-count crochet thread : #820 River Blue or #450 Aqua (A), #422 Golden Yellow (B); eyes are Mill Hill seed beads

GAUGE CIRCLE
(see page 7) = ⅜"/1cm worked on 2.00mm (size 4 steel U.S.) hook

FINISHED MEASUREMENT
Bird body only (#10 crochet cotton): 2½"/6.5 cm x 1⅜"/3.5 cm (beak and legs add variable height and width)

Lion Brand LB Collection Cotton Bamboo (52% Cotton, 48% Rayon from Bamboo; 3.5oz/100g = 245yd/224m) light weight yarn (3): #487-107 Hyacinth (A), #487-170 Gardenia (B); eye is a French knot made with No. 10 crochet cotton

GAUGE CIRCLE
(see page 7) = 1"/2.5cm worked on 4.00mm (size G-6 U.S.) hook

FINISHED MEASUREMENT
Bird body only (light weight yarn): 4¾"/12 cm x 2½"/6.5 cm (beak and legs add variable height and width)

INSTRUCTIONS

LEFT-FACING BIRD

With A, ch 10.

Row 1 (RS): Sc in 2nd ch from hook, hdc in next ch, dc in next ch, htr in next ch, tr in next ch, htr in next ch, dc in next ch, hdc in next ch, (2 sc, 2 hdc) in last ch. Do not turn. Instead, rotate the piece to work across opposite side of foundation ch, hdc in next free lp (it has an hdc in it already), hdc in each of next 7 ch-sts, PM in the last ch after working into it.

Row 2: To begin head, ch 8, 2 dc in 4th ch from hook, hdc in next ch, sc in each of next 3 ch, sc in next marked ch, remove marker.

Note: If the bird will be standing, you may want to define its wing. To do that, work the instructions bet [ ] in BLO. If it will be flying, work sts as usual and ignore [ ].

Row 3: Continuing around the bird's belly, working along the sts of Row 1, [sc in next sc, (sc, hdc) in next hdc, 2 dc in next dc, dc in next htr, 2 dc in next tr, dc in next htr, 2 dc in next dc, dc in next hdc, 2 dc in each of next 2 sc], dc in next hdc, PM in last hdc after working into it.

Row 4: To make bottom tail feather, ch 9, sc in 3rd ch from hook, hdc in next ch, dc in next ch, hdc in each of next 2 ch, sc in each of next 2 ch, ch 2, sl st in marked hdc at end of Row 3, remove marker, turn.

Row 5: To work top tail feather, ch 1, working back along the tail feather, sc in each of next 2 ch sts, sc in each of next 4 sts, ch 5, turn, sc in 3rd ch from hook, hdc in next ch, dc in next ch, hdc in each of next 2 sc, sc in each of next 4 sc.

Row 6: Working across the top of the bird, hdc in next 9 hdc.

Row 7: To finish bird's head, work into the free lps along the bird's neck as follows: hdc in each of 4 ch, 2 hdc in next ch, sk next ch, 2 hdc in each of next 2 ch, 3 hdc

in next dc, 2 hdc in next dc, working down the bird's neck, sc in next st, sc2tog over next 2 sts, sc in each of next 2 sts, cut yarn and needle-join to next st.

Singing beak for left-facing bird

This takes up 3 sts of the bird's head. Determine where you want the beak to be and with RS facing, join B with a sl st in appropriate st of the bird's head, ch 4, sl st in 2nd ch from hook, sc in next ch, hdc in last ch, sl st in next st of bird's head, ch 3, sl st in 2nd ch from hook, sc in next ch, sl st in next st of bird's head. Fasten off B.

RIGHT-FACING BIRD

With A, ch 11.

Row 1: (Hdc, 2 sc) in 3rd ch from hook (forming a ch-2 lp at the beginning of the row), working along ch, hdc in next ch, dc in next ch, htr in next ch, tr in next ch, htr in next ch, dc in next ch, hdc in next ch, 2 sc in last ch. PM in last ch after you work into it. Do not turn.

Row 2: To begin bird's head, ch 9, dc2tog over 4th and 5th ch from hook, hdc in next ch, sc in each of next 3 ch.

Row 3: Now you are looking at the free lps at the base of the original foundation ch. Hdc in next marked ch, remove marker, hdc in each of the next 7 ch of foundation ch, sk 1 ch of ch-2 lp at beg of Row 1, sl st in next ch-st, rotate work so you can work into the sts of Row 1.

Note: If the bird will be standing, you may want to define its wing. To do that, work the instructions bet [ ] in BLO. If it will be flying, work sts as usual and ignore [ ].

Row 4: Continuing around the bird's belly, working along the sts from Row 1, ch 2, dc in next hdc, PM in this dc, [2 dc in each of next 2 sc, dc in next hdc, 2 dc in next dc, dc in next htr, 2 dc in next tr, dc in next htr, 2 dc in next dc, (hdc, sc) in next hdc, sc in next sc].

Row 5: To finish the bird's head, sc in next sc, working in free lps of the original ch of the bird's neck, sc in next ch, sc2tog over next 2 ch, sc in next ch, 2 hdc in next ch, 3 hdc in next ch, sk 1 ch, 2 hdc in each of next 2 ch, 2 hdc in next dc, hdc in each of next 4 sts.

Row 6: Working across bird's back, hdc in each of next 8 sts, hdc in each of next 2 ch, PM in last hdc.

Row 7: To make the bird's tail, ch 9, sc in 3rd ch from hook, working along ch, hdc in next ch, dc in next ch, hdc in each of next 2 ch, sc in each of next 2 ch, sl st into the side of the hdc with marker in it, remove marker; ch 1, turn. Working back along the tail feather, sc in each of next 4 sts, ch 5, turn. Working back along tail feather toward the bird, sc in 3rd ch from hook, hdc in next ch, dc in next ch, hdc in each of next 2 sc, sc in each of next 2 sc, sl st in marked dc (from Row 4), remove marker. Fasten off.

Singing beak for right-facing bird

This takes up 3 sts of the bird's head. Determine where you want the beak to be and with RS facing, join B with a sl st in appropriate st on bird's head, ch 3, sl st in 2nd ch from hook, sc in next ch, sl st in next st of bird's head, ch 4, sl st in 2nd ch from hook, sc in next ch, hdc in last ch, sl st in next st of bird's head. Fasten off B.

Closed beak for either bird

This takes up 2 sts of the bird's head. Determine where you want the beak to be and with RS facing, join B with a sl st in appropriate st on bird's head, ch 4, sl st in 2nd ch from hook, sc in next ch, hdc in last ch, sl st in next st of bird's head. Fasten off B.

LEGS AND FEET (OPTIONAL)

Decide whether bird will be standing or running, then consult the photos to see where you want to attach the legs. For each leg/foot, with RS facing, join B with a sl st in appropriate st, ch 5, [ch 4, sl st in 2nd ch from hook, sl st in each of next 2 ch] 3 times, sl st in each ch of beg ch-5. Fasten off, and pull thread through the st along the bird's belly toward the back.

WING (OPTIONAL)

With A, ch 10. Sc in 2nd ch from hook, hdc in next ch, dc in next ch, htr in next ch, tr in next ch, htr in next ch, dc in next ch, hdc in next ch, sc in next ch. Fasten off, or for really beautiful results, cut yarn and needle-join to first ch-st of wing.

Make another wing if desired.

FINISHING

Weave in ends. Embroider eye or sew on a bead for eye. For flying bird, don't crochet feet. Instead, sew one wing to the front of the bird and one peeking out from under the bird, using the photo as a guide for placement.

turtle

My husband Charles brought home a turtle. We admired it before it retired into its shell. After a moment of distraction, the turtle was nowhere to be found. Turtles can go fast, if they want to.

SKILL LEVEL
Intermediate

MATERIALS & TOOLS
2 or more colors of yarn: Main color (A), accent color or colors (B)

Crochet hook: Appropriate size hook to achieve a firm gauge with selected yarn

Tapestry needle

PATTERN NOTE
Instructions are written for two colors of yarn, but you can use a different color for every row.

ABBREVIATIONS
Find instructions on pages 16 and 17 for: htr, sc-picot, dc2tog, dc-hdc-sctog

FOR THESE TURTLES WE USED

Cascade Ultra Pima Fine (100% pima cotton; 1.75oz/50g = 136.7yd/125m) sport weight yarn (2): #3744 Forest Green (A), #3762 Spring Green and #3740 Sprout (B).

GAUGE CIRCLE
(see page 7) = ¾"/2cm worked on 3.50mm (size E-4 U.S.) hook

FINISHED MEASUREMENT
3⅞"/9.8cm x 3⅞"/9.8cm for sea turtle

Cascade 220 Sport (100% Peruvian Highland wool; 1.75oz/50g = 164yd/15m) light weight yarn (3): #2409 Palm (A), #7808 Purple Hyacinth (B).

GAUGE CIRCLE
(see page 7) = ⅞"/2.2cm worked on 3.50mm (size E-4 U.S.) hook

FINISHED MEASUREMENT
3⅜"/8.5cm x 4⅜"/11.1cm for land turtle

Classic Elite Yarns Liberty Wool (100% washable wool; 1¾oz/50g = 122yd/111m) DK/sport weight yarn (3): #7818 Fresh Clay (A), #7836 Taupe and #7835 Citronella (B).

GAUGE CIRCLE
(see page 7) = ⅞"/2.2cm worked on 4.00mm (size G-6 U.S.) hook

FINISHED MEASUREMENT
4¼"/11cm x 4⅜"/11.1cm for sea turtle

INSTRUCTIONS

TURTLE

With A, ch 5, join with sl st to form ring.

Rnd 1: Ch 3 (counts as dc), 11 dc in ring, join with a sl st to top of beg ch-3. Fasten off A—12 sts.

Rnd 2: With RS facing, join B with hdc in any st of Rnd 1, ch 1, (tr, ch 1, hdc) in same st as first hdc, ch 1, sk next st, *(hdc, ch 1, tr, ch 1, hdc) in next st, ch 1, sk next st; rep from * 4 times, join with a sl st in first st of rnd—36 sts. Fasten off B. Skipped stitches are "free" sts.

Rnd 3: Fold Rnd 2 to back of work and out of the way. With RS facing, join A with *dc in next free st of Rnd 1, sk next hdc of Rnd 2, sc in BL of next ch-1, (sc, ch 1, sc) in BL of next st (this forms a point), sc in BL of next ch-1, sk next hdc; rep from * 5 times, sl st in first st of rnd, fasten off A—36 sts in the form of a 6-point star.

Rnd 4: Working in BLO, join B with *sc in ch-1 at tip of point, sc in next sc, hdc in next sc, 2 dc in next st, hdc in next st, sc in next st; rep from * 5 times, sl st in first sc—42 sts. Fasten off B.

For Turtle with Legs

Rnd 5: Work into BLO of Rnd 4. Find any 3 sc in a row in Rnd 4, insert hook into first of these, draw up lp;

HEAD

Ch 8, htr in 4th ch from hook, working down ch toward shell, htr in each of next 2 ch, dc in each of next 2 ch, sk next st of Rnd 4, sl st in next st;

Sl st in next 2 sts;

FIRST FRONT LEG

Ch 4, (slst-picot) 3 times, yo, draw up lp in base of 2nd picot, sk next picot, draw up lp in next ch (4 lps on hook), finish as htr, working down ch, dc2tog over next 2 ch, hdc in next ch, sk next st of Rnd 4, sl st in next st;

Sl st in next 8 sts;

FIRST HIND LEG

Work same as first front leg, above;

TAIL

Sl st in next 5 sts, ch 6, sl st in 2nd ch from hook, working down ch toward shell, sl st in next ch, sc in next 2 ch, hdc in next ch; sk next st of Rnd 4, sl st in next st;

Sl st in next 4 sts;

SECOND HIND LEG

Ch 3, (slst-picot) 3 times, yo, draw up lp in base of 2nd picot, sk next picot, draw up lp in next ch-st (4 lps on hook), finish as htr, 2 dc in next st, hdc in next st; sk next st of Rnd 4, sl st in next st;

Sl st in next 8 sts;

SECOND FRONT LEG

Work same as second hind leg, above;

Sl st in next 2 sts, sl st in next st which is beg of rnd, working across opposite side of foundation ch of head, sl st in next 5 ch, [ch 2, sc in next ch-3 space] twice, ch 2, working down toward shell, sl st in next 5 sts; cut yarn and needle-join to st at base of neck OR sl st into st at base of neck and fasten off A.

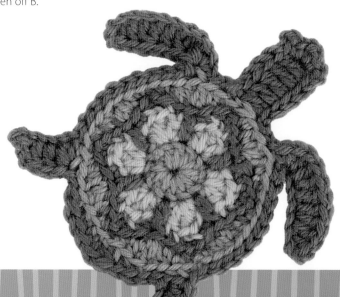

For Turtle with Flippers

Rnd 5: Work into BLO of Rnd 4. Find any 3 sc in a row in Rnd 4, insert hook into first of these, draw up lp;

HEAD

Ch 8, htr in 4th ch from hook, working down ch toward shell, htr in next 2 ch, dc in next 2 ch; sk next st of Rnd 4, sl st in next st;

Sl st in next 2 sts;

FIRST FRONT FLIPPER

Ch 12, working back along ch toward shell, hdc in 3rd ch from hook, dc in next ch, dc2tog over next 2 ch, dc in next ch, dc2tog over next 2 ch, dc-hdc-sctog over next 3 ch; sl st in next st of Rnd 4;

Sl st in next 10 sts;

FIRST HIND FLIPPER

Ch 4, slst-picot, ch 2, sk next 2 ch, sk next picot, dc in next 2 ch, hdc2tog over next 2 ch, sk next st of Rnd 4, sl st in next st of Rnd 4;

TAIL END

Sl st in next st, sc in next 2 sts, hdc in next st, 2 hdc in next st, hdc in next st, sc in next 2 sts, sl st in next 2 sts;

SECOND HIND FLIPPER

Ch 5, slst-picot, sk picot, sk next 2 ch, dc in next 2 ch, 2 hdc in last ch, sk next st of Rnd 4, sl st in next st of Rnd 4;

Sl st in next 10 sts;

SECOND FRONT FLIPPER

Ch 8, working back along ch toward shell, hdc in 3rd ch from hook, *dc in next ch, 2 dc in next ch; rep from * once, (dc, hdc, sc) in last ch, sl st in next st of Rnd 4;

Sl st in next st, sl st in next st which is beg of rnd, working across opposite side of foundation ch, up side of head, sl st in next 5 ch, [ch 2, sc in next ch-3 space] twice, ch 2, working down toward shell, sl st in next 5 sts; cut yarn and needle-join to st at base of neck OR sl st into st at base of neck and fasten off A.

FINISHING

Weave in ends; block.

lamb

"Does steel wool come from sheep?" my husband asked our daughter. "No, Dad," she said. He is so silly. Their conversation inspired the stainless steel yarn version of this little lamb.

SKILL LEVEL
Intermediate

MATERIALS & TOOLS
1 or 2 colors of yarn as desired: Body color (A), legs and head color (B)

Crochet hook: Appropriate size hook to achieve a firm gauge with selected yarn

Tapestry needle

ABBREVIATIONS
Find instructions on pages 16 and 17 for: FL, FLO, BLO, slst-picot, sc2tog

FOR THESE LAMBS WE USED
Berroco Ultra Alpaca Light (50% super fine alpaca, 50% Peruvian wool; 1.75oz/50g = 144yd/133m) sport weight yarn (2): #4201 Winter White (A), #4279 Potting Soil Mix (B).

GAUGE CIRCLE
(see page 7) = ⅞"/2.2cm worked on 3.75mm (size F-5 U.S.) hook

FINISHED MEASUREMENT
2¼"/5.5cm x 2½"/6.5cm excluding head

Lion Brand LB Collection Wool Stainless Steel (75% wool, 25% stainless steel; 0.5oz/14g = 273yd/244m) fingering 10-count crochet thread (0): #108 Dusty Blue (A) and (B).

GAUGE CIRCLE
(see page 7) = ⅜"/1cm with a triple strand worked on 2.00mm (size 4 steel U.S.) hook

FINISHED MEASUREMENT
1¼"/3.2cm x 1½"/3.8cm excluding head

INSTRUCTIONS

LAMB

With A, ch 6.

Rnd 1: 3 sc in 2nd ch from hook, sc in each of next 3 ch, 3 sc in last ch, rotate piece to work across opposite side of foundation ch, sk ch with 3 sc-sts already in it, sc in each of next 3 ch, join with sl st to FL of first sc—12 sc.

Rnd 2: Working in FLO of sts in Rnd 1, slst-picot, sl st in same st as join, *[slst-picot, sl st into next sc] twice, [slst-picot, sk 1 sc, sl st in next sc] twice; rep from * once—9 picots.

Rnd 3: Take a moment to look at the wrong side of work and identify the 12 back lps of Rnd 1. Turning back to the right side of piece, working in BLO of Rnd 1, ch 1, *2 sc in each of next 3 sc, sc in each of next 3 sc; rep from * once, join with sl st to FL of first sc—18 sc.

Rnd 4: Working in FLO of Rnd 3, *[slst-picot, sl st into next sc] 3 times, [slst-

picot, sk next sc, sl st in next sc] 3 times; rep from * once, join with sl st to first sc—12 picots.

Rnd 5: Take a moment to look at the wrong side of work and identify the 18 back lps of Rnd 3. Turning back to the right side of piece, working in BLO of Rnd 3, ch 1, *2 sc in each of next 6 sc, sc in each of next 3 sc; rep from * once, join with sl st to first sc—30 sc.

Rnd 6: Working in FLO of Rnd 5, *slst-picot, sk 1 st, sl st in next st; rep from * 14 times—15 picots. Fasten off.

Legs

Find the 5th picot of Rnd 6, fold it out of the way to the front, insert hook into BL of st behind picot, draw up lp of B, *ch 8, sl st in 3rd ch from hook, ch 3, sl st in 3rd ch from hook, sl st in rem 5 ch-sts, sl st in next st of body (first leg finished), ch 8, sl st in 3rd ch from hook, ch 3, sl st in 3rd ch from

hook, sl st in rem 5 ch-sts, sl st in same st of body. Fasten off.* Sk 3 sts of body, insert hook in BL of next st, draw up lp of B; rep from * to *.

Head

With A or B, ch 3, sc in 2nd ch from hook, 2 sc in next ch (ear complete), ch 6, hdc in 4th ch from hook, hdc in next ch, sc in next ch (face complete), ch 4, sc in 2nd ch from hook, sc2tog over next 2 ch-sts, sc in side of last sc of lamb's face. For best results, cut yarn and needle-join to first ch-st of piece; otherwise, join with sl st to first ch of piece. Fasten off.

FINISHING

For stainless steel blend yarn, do not block; instead, straighten each picot, ear, and leg, and arrange legs. For most other yarns (see "Read Me First," page 12, for advice), block lamb's legs and head. Use yarn ends to sew head to body, using photos as a guide for placement. Weave in ends.

underwater butterfly

Butterfly, surgeon, parrot, clown, and soap: What do they have in common? They're all names of reef fish. Colors, patterns, and shapes of reef creatures inspire crafters all over the world.

SKILL LEVEL
Intermediate

MATERIALS & TOOLS
3 colors of yarn: Body color (A), fin color (B), scrap of dark yarn for eye (C)

Scraps of yarn in different colors to add interest to eyes or fins

Crochet hook: Appropriate size hook to achieve a firm gauge with selected yarn

Tapestry needle

PATTERN NOTE
The four fish swimming above are made from one multicolor skein of yarn. It's a great way to color coordinate the whole school.

ABBREVIATIONS
Find instructions on pages 16 and 17 for: htr, sc-picot

FOR THESE FISH WE USED

Plymouth Yarn Company Kudo (55% cotton, 40% rayon, 5% silk; 3.5oz/100g = 198yd/180m) medium weight yarn : #56 multicolor brown, red, orange, yellow, gray, black (divided for A, B, and C).

GAUGE CIRCLE
(see page 7) = 1³⁄₁₆"/3cm worked on 5.00mm (size H-8 U.S.) hook

FINISHED MEASUREMENT
4"/10cm x 4"/10cm

Cascade 220 Sport (100% Peruvian Highland wool; 1.75oz/50g = 164yd/150m) light weight yarn : #8505 White (A), #7827 Goldenrod (B), #8555 Black (C).

GAUGE CIRCLE
(see page 7) = ⁷⁄₈"/2.2cm worked on 3.50mm (size E-4 U.S.) hook

FINISHED MEASUREMENT
3"/7.5cm x 2⁷⁄₈"/7.3cm

INSTRUCTIONS

BUTTERFLY FISH

With A, ch 5, join with sl st to form ring.

Rnd 1: Ch 2 (counts as hdc), 11 hdc in ring, join with sl st to top of beg ch-2—12 hdc.

Rnd 2: Ch 2 (counts as hdc), hdc in same st as sl st of prev rnd, 2 hdc in next 9 sts, hdc in next st, (dc, htr, dc) in next st, join with sl st to top of beg ch-2—24 sts.

Rnd 3: Ch 2 (counts as hdc), *2 hdc in next st, hdc in next st; rep from * 9 times, 2 hdc in next dc, dc in next htr, sc-picot, sc in side of dc just made, hdc in same st as dc, hdc in next dc; cut yarn and needle-join to first hdc of rnd OR join with sl st to top of beg ch-2. Fasten off A.

Rnd 4: Sk ch-2 at beg of Rnd 3, sk next 2 hdc, working in BLO of sts in Rnd 3, join B with sl st in next hdc;

Small lower fin

Ch 5, sl st in 2nd ch from hook, sc in next ch, sc2tog over next 2 ch, sl st in next st of Rnd 3;

Big lower fin

Sc in next st, 2 sc in next st, hdc in next st, (hdc, dc) in next st, htr in next st, tr in next st, ch 4, hdc in 3rd ch from hook, dc in next ch, sl st in same st of Rnd 3 as tr, sl st in next 2 sts;

Tail

Ch 2, hdc in each of next 2 sts, turn; ch 2, hdc in first hdc, hdc in next st, hdc in top of ch-2, turn; slst-picot, sl st in first hdc, sl st in next 2 sts, slst-picot, sl st in top of ch-2, rotate piece to work down side of tail, work 2 sl sts down side of tail, sl st in same st of Rnd 3 as beg hdc of tail, sl st in next 2 sts;

Top fin

Ch 2, dc in next st, (htr, tr) in next st, (tr, htr) in next st, 2 dc in next st, dc in each of next 5 sts, (2 hdc) in next st, sc in next st; sl st in next st and fasten off B OR cut yarn and needle-join to next st.

For a Butterfly Fish swimming in the other direction, make body through Rnd 3 as above.

Other direction Rnd 4: Sk ch-2 at beg of Rnd 3, sk next 2 hdc, working in BLO of sts in Rnd 3, join B with sl st in next hdc;

Top fin

Sc in next st, 2 hdc in next st, dc in each of next 5 sts, 2 dc in next st, (htr, tr) in next st, (tr, htr) in next st, dc in next st, ch 2, sl st in next 2 sts;

Tail

Ch 2, hdc in next 2 sts, turn; ch 2, hdc in first hdc, hdc in next st, hdc in top of ch-2, turn; slst-picot, sl st in first hdc, sl st in next 2 sts, slst-picot, sl st in top of ch-2, rotate piece to work down side of tail, work 2 sl sts down side of tail, sl st in same st of Rnd 3 as beg hdc of tail;

For Even More Fun...

Create your own aquarium by attaching thread to several of these fish, then hang in a real aquarium (sans water) decorated with plastic seaweed, colorful rocks, and colorful lighting. It's just as gorgeous as the real thing, plus you don't have to remember to feed them!

Big lower fin

Sl st in next 2 sts, ch 4, hdc in 3rd ch from hook, dc in next ch, tr in st with sl st in it, htr in next st, (dc, hdc) in next st, hdc in next st, 2 sc in next st, sc in next st;

Small lower fin

Sl st in next st, ch 4, sl st in 2nd ch from hook, sc in next ch, 2 sc in next ch; sl st in next st of Rnd 3 and fasten off B OR cut yarn and needle-join to next st of Rnd 3.

Eye

With C, ch 4, join with sl st to form ring.

Rnd 1: Ch 1, 6 sc in ring, join with sl st to first st of rnd, leaving a sewing length, join with sl st to first st of rnd and fasten off C OR cut yarn and needle-join to first st of rnd.

Body fin

With A, ch 4, hdc in 3rd ch from hook, sl st in next ch. Fasten off, leaving a sewing length.

FINISHING

Sew eye and body fin in place using photo as a guide. Weave in ends. Embroider details as desired.

bat

These mammals fly around at night with their webbed arms and fingers, using natural sonar to find their way. They sleep all day, upside down, with their webbed wings wrapped around them.

SKILL LEVEL
Intermediate

MATERIALS & TOOLS
1 color of yarn: Bat color (A)

Crochet hook: Appropriate size hook to achieve a firm gauge with selected yarn

Tapestry needle

Beads, buttons, or embroidery floss for eyes

PATTERN NOTE
Long picot = ch 4, sl st in 4th ch from hook.

ABBREVIATIONS
Find instructions on pages 16 and 17 for: dc2tog, joined-tr, slst-picot, st-top-picot

FOR THESE BATS WE USED

Classic Elite Yarns Woodland (65% wool, 35% nettles; 1¾oz/50g = 131yd/120m), DK weight yarn (3): #3154 Red Grape (A).

> **GAUGE CIRCLE**
> (see page 7) = 1"/2.5cm worked on 4.00mm (size G-6 U.S.) hook
>
> **FINISHED MEASUREMENT**
> 6¾"/17.1cm x 3⅜"/8.6cm

Plymouth Yarn Company Plymouth Select Worsted Merino Superwash (100% superwash fine merino wool; 3.5oz/100g = 218yd/198m) medium weight yarn (4): #42 Grape (A).

> **GAUGE CIRCLE**
> (see page 7) = 1"/2.5cm worked on 5.00mm (size H-8 U.S.) hook
>
> **FINISHED MEASUREMENT**
> 7¼"/18.4cm x 4¼"/10.8cm

INSTRUCTIONS

WINGS (MAKE 2)

With A, ch 1, make 2 long picots, sl st in base of first long picot, ch 17, make 2 long picots, sl st in base of first long picot, ch 1—19 ch, 4 long picots.

Row 1: Ch 3 (counts as first dc), 2 dc in 4th ch from hook, dc2tog inserting hook in base of picot for first st and in next ch for 2nd st, dc2tog over next 2 ch, hdc in next 3 ch, sc in next 5 ch, hdc in next 3 ch, dc2tog over next 2 ch, dc2tog inserting hook in next ch for first st and in base of picot for 2nd st, 3 dc in last ch, turn—21 sts.

Row 2: Ch 4 (counts as first tr), joined-tr in first st, 2 dc in next st, dc in next st, (dc, tr, dc) in next st, dc in next 2 sts, (dc, tr, dc) in next st, dc in next 7 sts, (dc, tr, dc) in next st, dc in next 2 sts, (dc, tr, dc) in next st, dc in next st, 2 dc in next st, 2 tr in next st, turn—33 sts.

Row 3: Ch 4 (counts as first st), slst-picot, joined-tr in first st, (2 dc) in next st, *[dc2tog over next 2 sts] twice, (2 dc, tr, st-top-picot, 2 dc) in next tr; rep from * once; dc2tog over next 2 sts, dc in next 5 sts, dc2tog over next 2 sts, **(2 dc, tr, st-top-picot, 2 dc) in next tr, (dc2tog over next 2 sts) twice; rep from ** once, 2 dc in next st, 2 tr in top of turning ch of prev row, st-top-picot, fasten off A—43 sts, 6 picots.

BODY

Ch 13.

Row 1: Hdc in 4th ch from hook, hdc in each of next 2 ch, dc in each of next 4 ch, sk next 2 ch, sl st in next ch.

Rnd 2: Ch 3, dc in same ch as sl st at end of prev rnd, 2 dc in each of next 2 ch, working across opposite side of foundation ch, 2 dc in next ch, dc in each of next 3 ch, hdc in each of next 3 ch, hdc in next ch, (hdc, dc, ch 2, dc, hdc) in next ch, hdc in next ch, hdc in next 3 sts, dc in next 3 sts, 2 dc in next st, join with sl st to top of ch-3 at beg of rnd.

Rnd 3: Make first ear: *Ch 3, dc2tog placing first st in same st as last sl st and placing 2nd st in next dc, ch 3, sl st in same st as 2nd dc of dec*, sl st in next 3 sts; rep from * to * once for 2nd ear, sl st in next 7 sts,

Make first foot: **Sl st in next st, (slst-picot) 3 times, sl st in same st**.

Tail section

Sl st in next 2 sts, sc in next st, (2 hdc, ch 2, 2 hdc) in next ch-2 sp, sc in next st, sl st in next 2 sts; rep bet ** to ** for 2nd foot, sl st in each remaining st to ear. Fasten off, leaving a long sewing length, cut yarn and needle-join to base of ear.

FINISHING

Sew body on top of wings as shown in photos. Weave in ends and block. Embroider or add buttons or beads for eyes. If desired, embroider further details.

oval owl

As featured in "Read Me First," page 5, these owl friends show that, when made from identical instructions, big yarn makes big owls, little thread makes little owls. "Please extrapolate this information to other motifs," they hoot, wisely.

SKILL LEVEL
Intermediate

MATERIALS & TOOLS
2 or 3 colors of yarn: Body and wing color (A), foot and eye color (B), pupil color (C)

Crochet hook: Appropriate size hook to achieve a firm gauge with selected yarn

Tapestry needle

PATTERN NOTE
Read about free lps on page 16.

FOR THESE OWLS WE USED

Lion Brand Nature's Choice Organic Cotton (100% organically grown cotton; 2.75oz/78g = 94 yd/86m) medium weight yarn (4): #201 Mocha (A), #099 Macadamia (B) and (C).

> **GAUGE CIRCLE**
> (see page 7) = 1⁷⁄₁₆"/3.6cm worked on 5.50mm (size I-9 U.S.) hook

> **FINISHED MEASUREMENT**
> 4⅜"/11.1cm x 6⅜"/16.2cm, with both wings down

Coats & Clark Aunt Lydia's Classic Crochet Thread, No. 10, Art. 154 (100% mercerized cotton, 350yd/320m, no weight given) 10-count crochet thread (0): #661 Frosty Green (A), #422 Golden Yellow (B), #484 Myrtle Green (C).

> **GAUGE CIRCLE**
> (see page 7) = ⅜"/1cm worked on 2.00mm (size 4 steel U.S.) hook

> **FINISHED MEASUREMENT**
> 2¾"/7cm x 2¼"/5.7cm, excluding antennae

INSTRUCTIONS

OWL

With A, ch 13.

Rnd 1: Dc in 4th ch from hook, dc in each of next 6 ch, sk next 2 ch, sl st in next ch—7 dc, 2 ch-3 lps.

Rnd 2: Ch 3 (counts as dc), dc in same st as sl st at end of last rnd, 2 dc in each of next 2 ch, working across opposite side of foundation ch, 2 dc in next ch, dc in each of next 5 ch, 2 dc in next ch, 2 dc in each of next 3 ch, working across top of Rnd 1, 2 dc in next dc, dc in next 5 dc, 2 dc in next dc, sl st to top of beg ch-3—30 dc.

Rnd 3: Ch 3 (counts as dc), dc in same st as sl st at end of last rnd, 2 dc in each of next 5 sts, dc in next 9 sts.

For first tuft

2 dc in next dc, ch 4, sc in 2nd ch from hook, sl st in next 2 ch (first feather made), ch 4, sc in 2nd ch from hook, sl st in next 2 ch, sl st in first ch of first feather, which already has a sl-st in it (2nd feather made), 2 hdc in same dc of Rnd 2;

Working across top of head, hdc in next st, sc in next 2 sts, hdc in next st;

For 2nd tuft

2 hdc in next dc, ch 4, sc in 2nd ch from hook, sl st in next 2 ch (first feather made), ch 4, sc in 2nd ch from hook, sl st in next 2 ch, sl st in first ch of first feather, which already has a sl-st in it (2nd feather made), 2 dc in same dc of Rnd 2;

To finish rnd, dc in next 9 sts, join with sl st to top of ch-3 at beg of rnd—42 sts, 2 sets of feathers. Fasten off A.

First foot

Join B with a sl st in 5th dc of Rnd 3, *ch 5, hdc in 3rd ch from hook, sc in next ch, sl st in next ch, sl st in same st of Rnd 3; rep from * twice. Fasten off B.

Second foot

Join B with a sl st in 3rd st from first foot, make another foot same as first foot.

Wings (make 2)

Row 1: With A, ch 7, sc in 3rd ch from hook (ch-2 lp formed), sc in next ch, hdc in next ch, sk 1 ch, sl st in next ch.

Rnd 2: Ch 1, 3 sc in same ch as sl st at end of previous rnd, 2 sc in next ch, working across opposite side of foundation ch, sc in each of next 3 ch, sc in next ch, sc-picot, sc in next ch, sc in next 3 sts on top of Row 1, join with a sl st in first sc of rnd, OR cut yarn and needle-join to first sc of rnd.

Eye and Beak

With B, ch 4, join with sl st to form ring.

Rnd 1: Ch 1, 7 sc in ring, join with a sl st to first sc.

Row 2: Ch 4, sc in 3rd ch from hook, hdc in next ch. Fasten off B.

Other Eye

With B, ch 4, join with sl st to form ring.

Rnd 1: Ch 1, 7 sc in ring, cut yarn and needle-join to first st of rnd, use yarn end to tack eye to top of final hdc of beak.

Antennae (require 2 sts on top of head)

Join C with sl st at top of head, *ch 6, (2 hdc, ch 2, sl st) in 3rd ch from hook, sl st in next 3 ch, sl st in same st of head,* sl st in next st; rep from * to * once, fasten off A.

FINISHING

Arrange wings as desired and sew to body. Sew eyes to body with C, with 6 or 7 sts coming from center of eye like spokes to just inside the outer rim of eye. Tack beak invisibly in place. Weave in ends and block.

MARTIANS ARE A HOOT

Late at night, by the light of the moon, Haneek the Martian owl loves to perch on a tree limb and admire the night sky. If humans appear, he quickly flies away, leaving them to wonder just what sort of owl has green feathers!

bunny

Hot pink is an amusing color for a bunny, but you may prefer more natural-looking muted browns and cream. Angora yarn is the ultimate natural choice for crocheting a bunny.

INSTRUCTIONS

BUNNY
With A, ch 7.

Row 1 (RS): Sc in 2nd ch from hook, sc in next 5 ch, ch 5, turn.

Rnd 2 (RS): 3 sc in 2nd ch from hook, 3 hdc in next ch, dc in next ch (1 ch-st remains unworked).

To make hind foot
Ch 5, sc in 2nd ch from hook, sc in next 2 ch, 3 sc in last ch, 2 dc in same ch as last dc, PM in the dc you just made.

Continuing along bunny's back, 3 dc in unworked ch-st, rotate piece to work along free lps of original foundation ch, 3 dc in first ch, dc in next 4 ch, 3 dc in next ch, rotate piece to work along top of Row 1 sts, 3 dc in each of next 2 sc, dc in next 4 sts, ch 2.

Rnd 3 (RS): Fold the hind foot out of the way toward the front, sl st into st with marker in it, remove marker, to make tail, (sl st, ch 4, tr-dctog, ch 2, sl st in 2nd ch from hook, ch 2, sl st) in next st, sl st in next 10 sts, PM in st with last sl st in it;

To make first ear
Ch 11, sl st in 3rd ch from hook, sl st in next ch, sc in next 4 ch, sl st in next ch (2 ch-sts remain unworked);

To make next ear
Ch 8, sl st in 3rd ch from hook, sl st in next ch, sc in next 3 ch, sl st in next ch;

To begin head
Draw up a lp in the last worked ch of first ear (it already has a sl st in it), draw up a lp in st with marker in it (3 lps on hook), (yo, draw through 2 lps) twice, dc in st with marker;

To finish head
Ch 4, sc in 3rd ch from hook, hdc in next ch, sl st in same st as marker, remove marker.

Continuing around bunny's chest, sl st in next 3 dc;

To make first front foot
Ch 5, sl st in 3rd ch from hook, sl st in next 2 ch, sl st in next dc;

To make next front foot
Ch 5, sl st in 3rd ch from hook, sl st in next 2 ch, sl st in same dc;

Continuing along bunny's tummy, sl st in next 4 dc, cut yarn, needle-join to next st, thread yarn end into tapestry needle, turn to WS, run needle and thread under back lps of first sc of hind foot, tack yarn to secure foot to body.

FINISHING
Weave in ends; block.

weiner dog

Did you know that dachshunds come in more sizes, colors, and types of coats than any other breed of dog? So feel free to experiment with your crocheted dachshund, using different colors and weights of yarn and different size hooks!

SKILL LEVEL
Intermediate

MATERIALS & TOOLS
1 or 2 colors of yarn: Dog color (A)

Crochet hook: Appropriate size hook to achieve a firm gauge with selected yarn

Tapestry needle

ABBREVIATIONS
Find instructions on pages 16 and 17 for: htr, PM, RM, RS, slst-picot

FOR THIS DOG WE USED
Berroco Ultra® Alpaca Light (50% super fine alpaca, 50% Peruvian wool; 1.75oz/50g = 144yd/133m) sport weight yarn (**2**): #4280 Mahogany Mix or #4279 Potting Soil Mix (A).

GAUGE CIRCLE
(see page 7) = ⅞"/2.2cm worked on 3.75mm (size F-5 U.S.) hook

FINISHED MEASUREMENT
4¼"/10.8cm wide x 2"/5.1 tall

INSTRUCTIONS

DOG

With A, ch 4, join with sl st to first ch to form ring.

Rnd 1 (RS): Ch 2, 11 hdc in ring, join with sl st in top of beg ch-2—12 hdc.

Rnd 2:

Start head

Ch 5, 2 dc in 4th ch from hook (this creates a ch-3 lp at end of head);

Make ear and finish head

Ch 6, hdc in 3rd ch from hook, dc in each of next 2 ch, ch 2, PM in 2nd ch from hook, sl st in last ch (ear finished), htr in same ch as last dc sts of head, 2 htr in next ch, sk next 2 sts of Rnd 1, sl st in next st;

Start body

Sc in next st, ch 12, hdc in 3rd ch from hook (this creates a 2-st turning ch), hdc in each of next 3 sts, dc in each of next 4 ch, htr in each of next 2 ch, sk next 2 sts of Rnd 1, sl st in next st;

Front leg and finish rnd

Ch 7, sc in 2nd ch from hook, sc2tog over next 2 ch, sc3tog over next 3 ch, sk next st of Rnd 1, sl st in next st, 2 sc in each of next 2 sts of Rnd 1, sl st in next st.

Rnd 3:

Under chin and nose

Sl st in each of 2 free lps of head, take a moment to identify the 3 sts of the ch-3 lp at end of head (first ch-st is probably pulled very tight), sl st in first ch-st of ch-3 lp at end of head;

Nose

Ch 6, sl st in 2nd ch from hook, sk next ch, hdc in each of next 3 ch (nose made), sk next ch in ch-3 lp at end of head, sl st in next ch, 2 sc in first dc, sc in next dc;

Ear and back of neck

Fold ear out of the way to back of work and sc in next st of head, fold ear to RS as shown in photo, insert hook in st with marker, RM, insert hook in next st of head, yo and pull through all 3 lps on hook (sc2tog made), sl st in next htr, sl st in next sl st (which joins neck to Rnd 1), sc in next sc;

Back and tail

Working in opposite side of foundation ch of body, sc in first ch, sl st in next 9 ch, sl st in next ch, ch 8, sl st in 2nd ch from hook, sl st in each of next 2 ch, 2 sl sts in next ch, sl st in next 3 ch, sk next ch at end of body, sc in first hdc of body;

Back leg

Ch 4, sc in 3rd ch from hook (creating a sc-picot), ch 6, sc in 2nd ch from hook, sc2tog over next 2 ch, draw up lp in each of next 2 ch and side of last sc in sc-picot, yo and draw through all 4 lps on hook (sc3tog made), (hdc, dc, 2 htr) in next ch, sk next st of body, sl st in next st;

Chest and finish

Sc in each of next 7 sts, sl st in free lp of first ch at base of front leg and fasten off OR cut yarn and needle-join around free lp at base of front leg.

FINISHING

Weave in ends. Block.

glazed doughnut

I love how our local doughnut shop decorates glazed doughnuts with sprinkles in our school colors. Sprinkle your crocheted doughnut with sewn-on bugle beads or seed beads.

SKILL LEVEL
Easy

MATERIALS & TOOLS
2 colors of yarn: Doughnut color (A), glaze color (B)

Crochet hook: Appropriate size hook to achieve a firm gauge with selected yarn

Polyester fiberfill

Embroidery floss or beads for sprinkles, with beading needle and thread

Tapestry needle

PATTERN NOTE
All rnds are worked with RS facing.

ABBREVIATIONS
Find instructions on page 17 for: RS

FOR THESE DOUGHNUTS WE USED
Dale of Norway Falk (100% superwash wool; 1¾oz/50g = 116yd/106m) DK weight yarn (3): #2642 Sandalwood (A), #0017 Off-White or #4415 Pink (B).

Mill Hill beads for sprinkles

GAUGE CIRCLE
(see page 7) = 1"/2.5cm worked on 4.00mm (size G-6 U.S.) hook

FINISHED MEASUREMENT
2¼"/5.7cm across x 1"/2.5cm tall

INSTRUCTIONS

DOUGHNUT

With A, ch 24, join with sl st in first ch to form ring.

Rnd 1 (RS): Ch 2 (counts as first hdc here and throughout), sk first ch, hdc in each ch around, join with sl st to top of beg ch-2—24 hdc.

Rnd 2: Ch 2, *2 hdc in next st, hdc in each of 2 next sts; rep from * 6 times, 2 hdc in next st, hdc in next st, join with sl st to top of ch-2 at beg of rnd—32 hdc.

Rnd 3: Ch 2, hdc in next st, *hdc2tog over next 2 sts, hdc in each of next 2 sts; rep from * 6 times, hdc2tog over next 2 sts, join with sl st to top of beg ch-2—24 sts.

Rnd 4: Ch 2, *hdc2tog over next 2 sts, hdc in next st; rep from * 6 times, hdc2tog over next 2 sts, join with sl st to top of beg ch-2—16 sts.

Rnd 5: Ch 2, [hdc2tog over next 2 sts] 8 times, sk beg ch-2, join with a sl st in next hdc—8 hdc.

Rnd 6: Ch 2, hdc in first st, 2 hdc in each of next 7 sts, join with sl st to top of beg ch-2—16 hdc. Fasten off, leaving a long sewing length. Don't worry, it isn't supposed to look like a doughnut yet.

Glaze

With B, ch 20, join with sl st to first ch to form ring.

Rnd 1 (RS): Ch 2, *2 hdc in next ch, hdc in next 3 sts; rep from * 3 times, 2 hdc in next st, hdc in next 2 sts, join with sl st to top of beg ch-2—25 hdc.

Rnd 2: *Sk next st, 5 dc in next st, sk next st, sl st in next 2 sts; rep from * 4 times, omitting last sl st, leaving a long sewing length, needle-join to first st of rnd—5 shells.

FINISHING

Turn doughnut piece with RS to inside. Bring together original ch (24 sts) with final rnd (16 sts). (Sew tog 1 st of original ch and 1 st of final rnd) twice, *sk 1 st of original ch, [sew tog next st of original ch and next st of final rnd] twice; rep from * around, stuffing lightly with fiberfill as you sew. Tack yarn. Weave in ends.

If desired, sew short embroidery sts, or sew bugle or seed beads to glaze to represent sprinkles. With doughnut seam-side down, sew glaze to top of doughnut. Weave in ends.

kiwi

At first glance, the brown, fuzzy outside of a kiwi doesn't seem too promising. Once you've seen the striking colors and pattern inside and tasted its bright flavor, you'll know that you can't always judge a fruit by its cover.

SKILL LEVEL
Intermediate

MATERIALS & TOOLS
3 colors of yarn: White or off-white (A), green (B), brown (C)

Black embroidery floss or beads to represent seeds, with needle and sewing thread

Crochet hook: Appropriate size hook to achieve a firm gauge with selected yarn

Tapestry needle

ABBREVIATIONS
Find instructions on page 16 for: BL, BLO, htr

FOR THESE KIWIS WE USED

Lion Brand LB Collection Cotton Bamboo (52% cotton, 48% rayon from bamboo; 3.5oz/100g = 245yd/224m) light weight yarn (3): #098 Magnolia (A), #174 Snapdragon (B), #126 Chocolate Dahlia (C); Anchor cotton embroidery floss for embellishment.

GAUGE CIRCLE
(see page 7) = 1"/2.5cm worked on 4.00mm (size G-6 U.S.) hook

FINISHED MEASUREMENT
2⅝"/6.6cm x 2¼"/5.7cm

Dale of Norway Falk (100% superwash wool; 1¾oz/50g = 116yd/106m) DK weight yarn (3): #0017 Off-White (A), #8817 Lime (B), #3072 Cocoa (C); Mill Hill beads for embellishment.

GAUGE CIRCLE
(see page 7) = 1"/2.5cm worked on 4.00mm (size G-6 U.S.) hook

FINISHED MEASUREMENT
2¼"/5.7cm x 2"/5cm

Berroco Ultra® Alpaca Light (50% superfine alpaca, 50% Peruvian wool; 1.75oz/50g = 144yd/133m) sport weight yarn (2): #4201 Winter White (A), #4275 Pea Soup Mix (B), #4279 Potting Soil Mix (C); Mill Hill beads for embellishment.

GAUGE CIRCLE
(see page 7) = ⅞"/2.2cm worked on 3.75mm (size F-5 U.S.) hook

FINISHED MEASUREMENT
2⅜"/6cm x 2"/5.1cm

INSTRUCTIONS

KIWI FRUIT

With A, ch 5, join with sl st to first ch to form a ring.

Rnd 1: Ch 1, *(3 sc, ch 1, sc, hdc, ch 2, hdc, sc, ch 1) in ring; rep from * once, join with sl st in first sc. Fasten off, leaving a 12"/31cm yarn end for embroidery OR cut yarn, leaving a similarly long yarn end and needle-join to first sc of rnd.

Rnd 2: Working in BLO (even when working into ch sts), join B with sc in first sc of Rnd 1, sc in next 2 sts, *sc in next ch, hdc in each of next 6 sts, sc in next ch*, sc in next 3 sts; rep from * to * once, join with a sl st in first sc.

Rnd 3: Ch 4 (counts as htr), htr in next 3 sts, 2 dc in each of next 6 sts, htr in next 5 sts, 2 dc in each of next 6 sts, htr in last sc; for loveliest results cut yarn and needle-join to top of ch-4 at beg of rnd OR join with sl st in top of ch-4 at beg of rnd and fasten off.

Rnd 4: Insert hook in BL of any st of Rnd 3, yo with D, and draw up a lp; working in BLO, sl st in each st around, loosening sts as necessary so they will go smoothly around ends of oval, and tightening sts so they will go smoothly along straighter edges of oval; cut yarn and needle-join to first st of rnd.

FINISHING

Use long end of A to embroider 6 to 12 straight lines radiating from outer edge of Rnd 1, using photo as a guide. Weave in ends. Embroider 13 French knot "seeds" or sew on 16 beads between each embroidered line.

> **For Even More Fun...**
> Stitch a few of these on a set of tea towels to give your kitchen a little fruit flavor!

ice cream cone

We always enjoyed meals with my husband's family. Why? My mother-in-law Gene's good cooking, for one thing, and also because my father-in-law, Bob, believed the proper conclusion to any meal was ice cream!

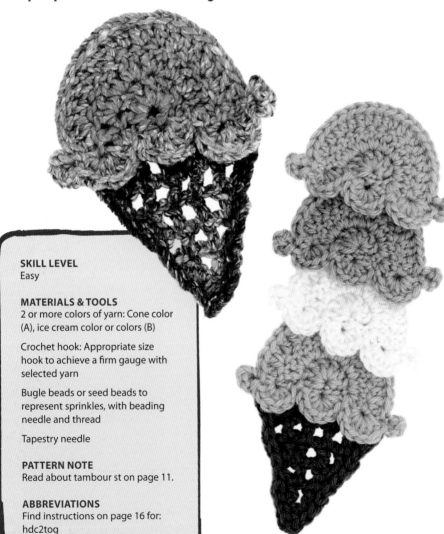

FOR THESE ICE CREAM CONES WE USED

Dale of Norway Falk (100% superwash wool; 1¾oz/50g = 116yd/106m) DK weight yarn (**3**): #3072 Cocoa (A), #4415 Pink, #0017 Off-White, and #2642 Sandalwood (B).

GAUGE CIRCLE
(see page 7) = 1"/2.5cm worked on 4.00mm (size G-6 U.S.) hook

FINISHED MEASUREMENT
3"/7.6cm x 3¾"/9.5cm for one scoop; 3"/7.6cm x 7"/17.8cm for four scoops

Lion Brand Nature's Choice Organic Cotton (100% organically grown cotton; 2.75oz/78g = 94yd/86m) medium weight yarn (**4**): #204 Limeade (A), #201 Mocha (B).

GAUGE CIRCLE
(see page 7) = 1⁷⁄₁₆"/3.6cm worked on 5.50mm (size I-9 U.S.) hook

FINISHED MEASUREMENT
4⅝"/11.7cm x 5⅝"/14.3cm

Plymouth Yarn Company Kudo (55% cotton, 40% rayon, 5% silk; 3.5oz/100g = 198yd/180m) medium weight yarn (**3**): #58 pink/burgundy/brown mix (A) and (B). Note: Use brown section for cone, pink section for ice cream.

GAUGE CIRCLE
(see page 7) = 1³⁄₁₆"/3.1cm worked on 5.00mm (size H-8 U.S.) hook

FINISHED MEASUREMENT
3⅞/9.8cm x 5"/12.7cm

SKILL LEVEL
Easy

MATERIALS & TOOLS
2 or more colors of yarn: Cone color (A), ice cream color or colors (B)

Crochet hook: Appropriate size hook to achieve a firm gauge with selected yarn

Bugle beads or seed beads to represent sprinkles, with beading needle and thread

Tapestry needle

PATTERN NOTE
Read about tambour st on page 11.

ABBREVIATIONS
Find instructions on page 16 for:
hdc2tog

INSTRUCTIONS

CONE

Row 1: With A, ch 4, dc in 4th ch from hook, turn.

Row 2: Ch 3 (counts as dc here and throughout), dc in first dc, ch 1, sk next ch-st, 2 dc in next ch, turn—4 dc, 1 ch-1 sp.

Row 3: Ch 4 (counts as dc, ch 1 here and throughout), dc in next dc, ch 1, sk next ch, dc in next dc, ch 1, dc in top of beg ch-3, turn—4 dc separated by ch-1 spaces.

Row 4: Ch 3, dc in first dc, [ch 1, sk next ch, dc in next dc] twice, ch 1, sk next ch, 2 dc in top of turning ch, turn—6 dc, 3 ch-1 spaces.

Row 5: Ch 4, dc in next dc, [ch 1, sk 1 ch, dc in next dc] 3 times, ch 1, dc in top of beg ch-3, turn—6 dc separated by ch-1 spaces.

Row 6: Ch 3, dc in first dc, [ch 1, sk next ch, dc in next dc] 4 times, ch 1, sk next ch, 2 dc in top of turning ch—8 dc, 5 ch-1 spaces. Do not turn.

Outline: Rotate cone, work 10 to 12 tambour sts across right side edge to point, sl st into st at point of cone, ch 1, sl st into point again, rotate cone, work 10 to 12 tambour sts up left side of cone from point to top corner. Fasten off.

ICE CREAM SCOOP (MAKE 1 OR MORE)

With B, ch 5, join with sl st to form ring.

Row 1: Ch 3 (counts as dc here and throughout), 7 dc in ring, turn—8 dc.

Row 2: Ch 3, dc in first dc, 2 dc in each of next 6 dc, 2 dc in top of ch-3 at beg or Row 1, turn—16 dc.

Row 3: Ch 3, 2 dc in next dc, *dc in next dc, 2 dc in next dc; rep from * 5 times, dc in next st, dc in top of ch-3 at beg of Row 2—23 sts. Do not turn.

Trim row: Ch 3, (2 hdc, ch 1, sl st) in 3rd ch from hook, rotate piece to work along straight side of ice cream scoop;

First shell: 6 hdc in top of turning ch of Row 2 (this already has a st in it), sl st in last dc of Row 1 (this already has a st in it);

Second shell: 7 hdc in st of ch-5 ring at beg of Row 1 (this will probably be sl-st that joins ring), sl st in 3rd ch of ch-3 at beg of Row 1 (already has sts in it);

Third shell: 6 hdc in top of dc at end of Row 2, sl st in 3rd ch of ch-3 at beg of Row 3;

Last bit: Ch 4, hdc2tog over 3rd and 4th ch from hook, sl st in 3rd ch of ch-3 at beg of Row 3 (already has a sl st in it), leaving a long end for sewing, fasten off.

FINISHING

Using long yarn end, sew ice cream scoop to top of cone. Sew additional scoops to top of previous ice cream scoop. If desired, add sprinkles to your ice cream with bugle beads or seed beads. A tip for your next ice cream social: crocheted Martians apparently prefer pistachio flavor, as shown above.

homemade pie

Making pie has never been easier. The no-bake lattice pie crust is easy, and there's no fussy dough rolling and cutting. To change the pie filling, simply use a different color of yarn.

SKILL LEVEL
Intermediate

MATERIALS & TOOLS
3 colors of yarn: Pie filling color (A), pie lattice and crust color (B), pie tin color (C)

Crochet hook: Appropriate size hook to achieve a firm gauge with selected yarn

Polyester fiberfill

Tapestry needle

ABBREVIATIONS
Find instructions on pages 16 and 17 for: FPdc, BPdc, BLO, RS, WS

FOR THESE PIES WE USED

Lion Brand LB Collection Angora Merino (80% extra-fine merino wool, 20% angora; 1.75oz/50g = 131yd/120m) light weight yarn (3): #174 Avocado (A), #187 Nectarine (B), #150 Smoked Pearl (C).

GAUGE CIRCLE
(see page 7) = ⅞"/2.2cm worked on 4.00mm (size G-6 U.S.) hook

FINISHED MEASUREMENT
3"/7.6cm across x 1"/2.5cm tall

Cascade 220 Sport (100% Peruvian Highland wool; 1.75oz/50g = 164yd/15m) light weight yarn (3): #7802 Cerise (A), #8622 Camel (B), #9568 Twilight Blue (C).

GAUGE CIRCLE
(see page 7) = ⅞"/2.2cm worked on 3.50mm (size E-4 U.S.) hook

FINISHED MEASUREMENT
2½"/6.4cm across x ⅞"/2.2cm tall

INSTRUCTIONS

PIE FILLING

With A, ch 4, join with sl st in first ch to form ring.

Rnd 1: Ch 2, 11 hdc in ring, join with sl st to top of beg ch-2—12 hdc.

Rnd 2: Ch 2, hdc in first st, 2 hdc in each of next 11 sts, join with sl st to top of beg ch-2—24 hdc.

Rnd 3: Ch 2, *2 hdc in next st, hdc in next st; rep from * 10 times, 2 hdc in next st, join with sl st to top of beg ch-2—36 hdc. Fasten off A.

LATTICE TOP

With B, ch 10.

Row 1 (WS): Hdc in 7th ch from hook, ch 2, sk next 2 ch, (hdc, ch 2, tr) in next ch, turn.

Row 2: Ch 6 (counts as tr, ch 2), hdc in first tr, ch 2, FPdc around next hdc, ch 2, BPdc around next hdc, ch 2, sk next next 2 ch, (hdc, ch 2, tr) in next ch, turn.

Row 3: Ch 4 (counts as hdc, ch 2), sk next 2 ch, FPdc around next hdc, ch 2, BPdc around next dc, ch 2, FPdc around next dc, ch 2, BPdc around next hdc, ch 2, sk next 2 ch, hdc in next ch, turn.

Row 4: Ch 4 (counts as hdc, ch 2), sk next 2 ch, *BPdc around next dc, ch 2, FPdc around next dc, ch 2; rep from * once, sk next 2 ch, hdc in next ch, turn.

Row 5: Ch 4 (counts as tr), sk next 2 ch, FPdc around next dc, ch 2, BPdc around next dc, ch 2, FPdc around next dc, ch 2, BPdc-tr-tog placing first st around next dc, sk next 2 ch, place 2nd st in next ch, turn.

Row 6 (RS): Ch 4 (counts as tr), sk first st and next 2 ch, FPdc around next dc, ch 2, BPdc around next dc, ch 4, sk next 2 ch, sl st in top of next dc, ch 1, do not turn—14 sps around outside of lattice.

Rnd 7 (pie crust): Place pie filling, RS up, underneath lattice. In this rnd, you will join lattice to filling by stitching into spaces around edge of lattice and at the same time, working into each st of pie filling.

Insert hook into next ch-4 sp of lattice and into any st of last rnd of filling, pull up lp and complete sc, ch 2, [sc into same ch-3 sp and next st of filling, ch 2] twice.

Now that you have the idea of how this works, instructions will tell you how many sts to work into each sp around the edge of the lattice, and you will know that each st goes into the next st of filling. There will be 36 sc in all, to match 36 sts in last rnd of pie filling.

In 2nd sp (formed by the side of a dc), [sc, ch 2] twice.

In 3rd sp (formed by a turning ch), [sc, ch 2] twice.

In 4th sp (formed by a diagonal tr), [sc, ch 2] 3 times.

In 5th sp (formed by ch-4), [sc, ch 2] 3 times.

In ch-2 sp (formed by foundation ch), [sc, ch 2] twice.

In 7th sp (formed by diagonal tr), [sc, ch 2] 3 times. Halfway there!

In 8th sp (formed by ch-4), [sc, ch 2] 3 times.

In 9th sp (formed by the side of a dc), [sc, ch 2] twice.

In 10th sp (formed by a turning ch), [sc, ch 2] twice.

In 11th sp (formed by a diagonal tr), [sc, ch 2] 3 times.

In 12th sp (formed by ch-4), [sc, ch 2] 3 times.

In ch-2 sp at top of Row 6 of lattice, [sc, ch 2] twice.

In last ch-4 sp, [sc, ch 2] 3 times, join with sl st in first sc. Fasten off B, leaving a long sewing length OR leaving long end for sewing, cut yarn and needle-join last ch-st to first sc of rnd.

PIE TIN

With C, ch 4, join with sl st to first ch to form ring.

Rnd 1 (RS): Ch 2 (counts as hdc), 11 hdc in ring, join with sl st to top of beg ch-2 —12 hdc.

Rnd 2 (RS): Ch 2, hdc in first st, 2 hdc in each of next 11 sts, join with sl st to top of beg ch-2—24 hdc.

Rnd 3 (RS): Ch 1, *2 sc in next st, sc in next st; rep from * 11 times, join with sl st to first sc—36 sc.

Rnd 4: Ch 2 (counts as hdc), hdc in BL of next 35 sts, join with sl st in top of beg ch-2. Fasten off B, leaving a long sewing length OR leaving long end for sewing, cut yarn and needle-join last ch-st to first sc of rnd.

FINISHING

If desired, leave ends to stuff into pie. If not, weave in ends except for long sewing lengths.

With tapestry needle, weave sewing length of pie crust (Rnd 7) underneath pie filling, and bring it out at center top of pie lattice, let it hang there for now.

Examine WS of filling, where you will see the backs of 36 sc of pie crust, each one forming a V shape. Place WS of filling with WS of pie tin together. Sew pieces together with sewing length, skimming needle behind the V-shaped threads of the pie-crust-sc and through the BL of a st of pie tin. *Sew next V-shaped sc to next BL of pie tin; rep from * about 3/4 of way around pie, stuff very lightly with wisps of fiberfill, preserving almost-flat shape of pie, finish sewing seam.

Thread needle with yarn coming from top of pie, stitch down through pie, with needle emerging from center bottom, skim one or two lps at bottom center as invisibly as possible, bring needle back to top, adjust tension to preserve pie shape, tack yarn invisibly at top of pie, weave in end.

Weave in any rem ends.

squash trio

Add jack-o'-lantern features to any or all of these squashes because . . . hey, why should pumpkins have all the fun?

SKILL LEVEL
Intermediate

MATERIALS & TOOLS

3 colors of yarn: Squash color (A), stem color (B)

Crochet hook: Appropriate size hook to achieve a firm gauge with selected yarn

7 safety pins for pumpkin

Polyester fiberfill

Tapestry needle

A few yards (m) of black or yellow yarn or thread to embroider jack-o'-lantern features

Optional: Black or yellow embroidery floss for jack-o'-lantern detail

ABBREVIATIONS

Find instructions on pages 16 and 17 for: hdc2tog, sc2tog, WS

FOR THESE SQUASHES WE USED

Plymouth Yarn Company Plymouth Select Worsted Merino Superwash (100% superwash fine merino wool; 3.5oz/100g = 218yd/198m) medium weight yarn (4): #40 orange (A) (for pumpkin), #38 gold (A) (for butternut squash), #42 purple (B) (for stem).

GAUGE CIRCLE
(see page 7) = 1"/2.5cm worked on 5.00mm (size H-8 U.S.) hook

FINISHED MEASUREMENT
3"/7.6cm in diameter for pumpkin, excluding stem; 2"/5.1cm in diameter x 4"/10.2cm tall for butternut squash

Plymouth Yarn Company Mushishi (95% wool, 5% silk; 8.9oz/250g = 491yd/447) DK weight yarn (3): #07 Rust (A) and (B).

GAUGE CIRCLE
(see page 7) = 15/16"/2.4cm worked on 3.75mm (size F-5 U.S.) hook

FINISHED MEASUREMENT
2 5/8"/6.7cm in diameter for pumpkin, excluding stem

Cascade 220 Sport (100% Peruvian Highland wool; 1.75oz/50g = 164yd/15m) light weight yarn (3): #7825 Orange Sherbet (A), #8622 Camel (B).

GAUGE CIRCLE
(see page 7) = 7/8"/2.2cm worked on 3.50mm (size E-4 U.S.) hook

FINISHED MEASUREMENT
2"/5cm in diameter x 1"/2.5cm thick for scallop squash

INSTRUCTIONS

Stem for All Squashes

With B, ch 6, sc in 2nd ch from hook, sc in each ch across. Fasten off B, leaving a sewing length.

PUMPKIN

With A, ch 5, join with a sl st to form a ring.

Rnd 1: Ch 2 (counts as hdc here and throughout), 13 hdc in ring, join with sl st to top of beg ch-2—14 hdc.

Rnd 2: Ch 2, hdc in first st, 2 hdc in next st, ch 3, *2 hdc in each of next 2 sts, ch 3; rep from * 5 times, join with sl st to top of beg ch-2—28 hdc, 7 ch-lps.

Rnd 3: Ch 2, 2 hdc in next st, hdc in each of next 2 sts, ch 3, *sk next ch-sp, hdc in next hdc, 2 hdc in next st, hdc in each of next 2 sts, ch 3; rep from * 5 times, join with sl st to top of beg ch-2—35 hdc (7 sets of 5 hdc), 7 ch-lps.

Rnd 4: Sl st in next hdc, ch 2, hdc in next 2 sts, 2 hdc in next st, ch 3, *sk next ch-sp, sk first hdc, hdc in next 3 sts, 2 hdc in next st, ch 3; rep from * 5 times, join with sl st to top of beg ch-2—35 hdc, 7 ch-lps.

Rnd 5: Rep Rnd 4.

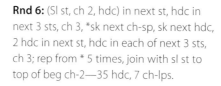

Rnd 6: (Sl st, ch 2, hdc) in next st, hdc in next 3 sts, ch 3, *sk next ch-sp, sk next hdc, 2 hdc in next st, hdc in each of next 3 sts, ch 3; rep from * 5 times, join with sl st to top of beg ch-2—35 hdc, 7 ch-lps.

Rnds 7 and 8: Rep Rnd 4.

Rnd 9: Rep Rnd 6.

Rnd 10: Sl st in next hdc, ch 2, hdc in next 3 sts, ch 3, *sk next ch-sp, sk next hdc, hdc in each of next 4 sts, ch 3; rep from * 5 times, join with sl st to top of beg ch-2—28 hdc, 7 ch-lps.

Rnd 11: Sl st in next hdc, ch 2, hdc in next 2 sts, ch 3, *sk next ch-sp, sk next hdc, hdc in each of next 3 sts, ch 3; rep from * 5 times, join with sl st to top of beg ch-2—21 hdc, 7 ch-lps.

Rnd 12: Sl st in next hdc, ch 2, hdc in next st, ch 3, *sk next ch-sp, sk first hdc, hdc in each of next 2 sts, ch 3; rep from * 5 times, join with sl st to top of beg ch-2, open last lp wide so it won't unravel as you work the next step (this is the active lp)—14 hdc, 7 ch-lps.

Turn piece inside out. The ch-3 lps will be prominent on this side. Counting from Rnd 2 to Rnd 12, you should have 11 ch-3 lps between each pair of hdc-segments. Working one section at a time, insert hook under the ch-3 lps of Rnd 2 and Rnd 3, pull Rnd 3's lp under Rnd 2's lp. *Insert hook under the lp of the next rnd and pull it under the previous ch-3 lp; rep from * until one ch-3 lp remains on hook, pin a safety pin through this lp to keep it from unraveling. Repeat process for each set of ch-3 lps—7 safety pins at top of piece.

Rnd 13: Turn piece RS out, insert hook into active lp and pull yarn to tighten lp to a working tension, ch 2, *insert hook into next ch-3 lp, remove safety pin, complete a sc into ch-3 lp, sk next hdc, hdc into next st; rep from * 4 times, sc in next ch-3 lp as before, join with sl st to beg ch-2—14 sts. Fasten off A.

Pumpkin Lid

With A, ch 5, join with a sl st in first ch to form ring.

Rnd 1 (WS): Ch 3 (counts as first dc), 13 dc in ring, join with sl st to top of ch-3 at beg of rnd—14 dc.

Rnd 2: *(Hdc, dc, hdc) in next st, sl st in next st; rep from * 6 times, leaving a long end for sewing—21 hdc, 7 sl st. Fasten off A.

FINISHING

Turn pumpkin lid WS up (the scallops lie better this way), sew stem to middle of pumpkin lid. Weave in all ends except long ends for sewing. Stuff pumpkin

lightly with polyester fiberfill. Sew lid to top of pumpkin. Add jack-o'-lantern features if desired.

BUTTERNUT SQUASH

With A, ch 4, join with a sl st in first ch to form ring.

Rnd 1: Ch 2 (counts as first hdc here and throughout), 9 hdc in ring, join with sl st to top of beg ch-2—10 hdc.

Rnd 2: Ch 2, hdc in next 3 sts, 2 hdc in next st, hdc in next 4 sts, 2 hdc in next st, join with sl st to top of beg ch-2—12 hdc.

Rnd 3: Ch 2, hdc in each st around, join with sl st to top of beg ch-2—12 hdc.

Rnds 4–7: Rep Rnd 3.

Rnd 8: Ch 2, *2 hdc in each of next 2 sts, hdc in next st; rep from * twice, 2 hdc in each of next 2 sts, join with sl st to top of beg ch-2—20 hdc.

Rnds 9 and 10: Ch 2, hdc in each st around, join with sl st to top of beg ch-2—20 hdc.

Rnd 11: Ch 2, [hdc2tog over next 2 sts] 10 times, sk beg ch-2, sl st in top of first hdc2tog—10 hdc. Stuff squash lightly with polyester fiberfill.

Rnd 12: Ch 1, starting in first st, [sc2tog over next 2 sts] 5 times, sl st in first sc2tog—5 sts. Fasten off, leaving a long sewing length.

FINISHING

Add more polyester fiberfill if needed. Use yarn end at bottom of squash to sew top closed. Sew stem to top of squash. Add jack-o'-lantern features if desired.

SCALLOP SQUASH

Top

With A, ch 4, join with a sl st to form a ring.

Rnd 1 (RS): Ch 2 (counts as first hdc), 9 hdc in ring, join with sl st to top of beg ch-2—10 hdc.

Rnd 2: Ch 2, hdc in first st, 2 hdc in each of next 9 sts, join with sl st to top of beg ch-2—20 hdc.

Rnd 3: Ch 1, sc in first st, *2 sc in next st, sc in next st; rep from * 8 times, 2 sc in last st, join with sl st in top of first sc—30 sc.

Rnd 4: *(Hdc, dc) in next st, (dc, hdc) in next st, sl st in next st; rep from * 9 times—10 scallops. Fasten off A.

Bottom

With A, ch 4, join with a sl st to form a ring.

Rnds 1 and 2: Rep Rnds 1 and 2 of scallop squash top. Fasten off, leaving a long sewing length.

FINISHING

Sew stem to center top of squash. Weave in ends except for sewing end. With WS together, sew 2 sts of top and bottom tog, *sk 1 st of top, sew next 2 sts of top and bottom tog; rep from * around, stuffing lightly with fiberfill before completely closing the seam. Embroider jack-o'-lantern features if desired.

cupcake

Icing is my favorite part of cake, whether it's buttercream frosting or the chocolate glaze on Sachertorte. Swirls of yarny frosting top these cupcakes. Hmmm ... is there any confectioners' sugar in the house?

For Even More Fun...
A cupcake embellishment sewn onto the front of a little girl's T will take her shirt from so-so to sweet!

SKILL LEVEL
Intermediate

MATERIALS & TOOLS
3 colors of yarn: Cake color (A), frosting color (B), cup color (C)

Crochet hook: Appropriate size hook to achieve a firm gauge with selected yarn

Tapestry needle

Straight pins

Optional: Embroidery floss or beads with thread and beading needle for decorations

ABBREVIATIONS
Find instructions on pages 16 and 17 for: BLO, FLO, htr, RS, WS, st-top-picot

FOR THESE CUPCAKES WE USED

Classic Elite Yarns Woodland (65% wool, 35% nettles; 1¾oz/50g = 131yd/100m) DK weight yarn (**3**): #3150 Sunshine (A), #3101 Ivory (B), #3195 Violet (C).

GAUGE CIRCLE
(see page 7) = 1"/2.5cm worked on 4.00mm (size G-6 U.S.) hook

FINISHED MEASUREMENT
2¾"/7cm x 4"/10.2cm

Dale of Norway Falk (100% superwash wool; 1¾oz/50g = 116yd/106m) DK weight yarn (**3**): #2611 Sand (A), #4416 Peony (B), #8817 Lime (C).

GAUGE CIRCLE
(see page 7) = 1"/2.5cm worked on 4.00mm (size G-6 U.S.) hook

FINISHED MEASUREMENTS
2⅝"/6.7cm x 4"/10.2cm

INSTRUCTIONS

CAKE

With A, ch 15.

Row 1 (RS): Dc in 4th ch from hook, htr in each of next 10 sts, (dc, ch 3, sl st) in last ch-st—12 sts, 2 ch-3 lps. Fasten off A.

ICING

Row 1 (RS): Draw up a lp of B in first htr of cake, ch 4, dc in 4th ch from hook, htr in same st as drawn-up lp, htr in each of next 2 sts, dc in each of next 2 sts, hdc in each of next 2 sts, sc in each of next 2 sts, sl st in next st, turn—10 sts, sl st, ch-3 lp.

Row 2 (WS): Ch 4, dc in 4th ch from hook, working across in FLO, htr in next sl st, htr in next st, dc in each of next 2 sts, hdc in each of next 2 sts, sc in each of next 2 sts, sl st in next st, turn—9 sts, sl st, ch-3 lp.

Row 3: Ch 4, dc in 4th ch from hook, working across in BLO, htr in next sl st, dc in next 2 sts, hdc in next 2 sts, sc in next 2 sts, sl st in next st, turn—8 sts, sl st, ch-3 lp.

Row 4: Ch 4, dc in 4th ch from hook, working across in FLO, htr in next sl st, dc in next st, hdc in next 2 sts, sc in next 2 sts, sl st in next st, turn—7 sts, sl st, ch-3 lp.

Row 5: Ch 3, working across in BLO, dc in next sl st, htr in next st, tr in next st, st-top-picot, htr in next st, dc in next st, (hdc, ch 2, sl st) in next st—6 sts, 1 picot, 2 ch-2 lps. Fasten off B.

CUP

With C, ch 10.

Row 1: Sl st in 3rd ch from hook (picot made), sc in across next 7 ch, turn—1 picot, 7 sc.

Row 2: Ch 1, sk first sc, working in BLO, sc in each of next 6 sts, slst-picot, turn—ch 1, 6 sc, 1 picot.

Row 3: Working in BLO, sc in each of next 6 sts, sc in next ch-st, turn—7 sc.

Row 4: Ch 1, sk first sc, working in BLO, sc in each of next 6 sts, slst-picot, turn—ch 1, 6 sc, 1 picot.

Rows 5–12: Repeat Rows 3 and 4 (4 times).

Row 13: Working in BLO, sc in each of next 6 sts, sl st in next ch-st—6 sc, 1 sl st. Fasten off C, leaving a long sewing length.

FINISHING

Weave in ends of cake and icing piece and block.

Weave long end of cup along non-picot end and pull together slightly. Tack end and weave in. Arrange picots along bottom edge of cake, spreading them out evenly across as in photo, pin in place. Sew picots to bottom edge of cake, remove pins.

If desired add beads or other embellishment.

cheese sandwich on a kaiser roll

My editors at Lark wanted all kinds of cookies, cupcakes, and doughnuts for this chapter. My motherly instincts kicked in. "Ladies, that's too much sugar!" I said. "Here, have a cheese sandwich, instead."

INSTRUCTIONS

BOTTOM BUN

With A, ch 4, join to first ch with sl st to form ring.

Rnd 1 (RS): Ch 2 (counts as hdc), 9 hdc in ring, join with sl st to top of beg ch-2 —10 hdc.

Rnd 2: Ch 2, hdc in first st, 2 hdc in each of next 9 hdc, join with sl st to top of beg ch-2—20 hdc.

Rnd 3: Ch 2, *2 hdc in next st, hdc in next st; rep from * 8 times, 2 hdc in next st, join with sl st to BL at top of beg ch-2—30 hdc.

Rnd 4: Ch 2, working in BLO, hdc in each st around, join with sl st to top of beg ch-2—30 hdc. Fasten off A.

Inside Bun

With B, ch 4, join to first ch with sl st to form ring.

Rnds 1–3: Work same as Rnds 1–3 of bottom bun. Fasten off B, leaving a long sewing length.

With WS together, sew bottom bun and inside bun together, inserting a wisp of fiberfill before closing seam completely. To keep piece flat, take yarn end inside bun toward its center. Dip needle to catch a lp of the bottom of the bun from the inside, bring it back out at the top side of the bun, and weave in end.

TOP BUN

With A, ch 4, join to first ch with sl st to form ring.

Rnd 1 (RS): Ch 1, [sc, ch 2] 5 times in ring, join with sl st to first sc—5 sc, 5 ch-2 sps.

Rnd 2: Ch 2 (counts as hdc), (3 hdc) in first st, ch 2, *(4 hdc) in next sc, ch 2; rep from * 3 times, sl st in top of beg ch-2—20 hdc, 5 ch-2 sps. To help you locate the ch-2 lps later, place a safety pin in each one.

Rnd 3: Sl st in each of next 2 hdc, ch 2 (counts as hdc here and throughout), 2 hdc in next hdc, 2 hdc in next ch-st, ch 3, *sk rest of ch-lp and next 2 hdc, hdc in next hdc, 2 hdc in next hdc, 2 hdc in next ch-st, ch 3; rep from * 3 times, join with sl st to top of beg ch-2—25 hdc, 5 ch-3 lps.

Rnd 4: Sl st in next 2 hdc, (sl st, ch 2, hdc) in next hdc, 2 hdc in next hdc, 2 hdc in next ch-st, ch 3, *sk rest of ch-lp and next 3 hdc, 2 hdc in each of next 2 hdc, 2 hdc in next ch-st, ch 3; rep from * 3 times, join with sl st to top of beg ch-2—30 hdc, 5 ch-3 lps.

Rnd 5: Sl st in next 3 hdc, ch 2, hdc in next hdc, 2 hdc in next hdc, 2 hdc in next ch-st, ch 3, *sk rest of ch-lp and next 3 hdc, hdc in next 2 hdc, 2 hdc in next hdc, 2 hdc in next ch-st, ch 3; rep from * 3 times, join with sl st to top of beg ch-2—30 hdc, 5 ch-3 lps.

Pull the last lp out wide so it won't come undone as you do next step. Turn to WS, find "ladders" created by ch-lps. Working up one ladder at a time, *transfer ch-2 lp of Rnd 1 (which has a safety pin in it) to larger hook. [Hook ch-3 lp of next rnd through the lp on hook] 3 times, insert safety pin into lp on hook to keep it from unraveling, remove hook from lp; rep from * for each ch-lp ladder. Turn to RS.

Rnd 6: Insert smaller hook in open lp at end of Rnd 5, tighten yarn around hook, sl st in next hdc, ch 2, hdc in each of next 4 hdc, hdc into lp with safety pin in it, remove safety pin, *sk next hdc, hdc in each of next 5 hdc, hdc in lp with safety pin in it, remove safety pin; rep from * 3 times, join with sl st to top of beg ch-2, cut yarn and needle-join—30 hdc.

Inside Bun

Make another inside bun piece, same as above, except leave a longer sewing length.

If desired, sew beads to top of roll, to resemble poppy seeds or other seeds. With WS of top bun and inside bun tog, use long end of B to sew pieces tog around their edges, stuffing lightly with polyester fiberfill before completely closing seam. To help preserve the shape of this piece, weave the B end to center of inside bun, take needle up through middle of top bun, then down again through inside bun, weave in end, invisibly.

TOMATO SLICE

With C, ch 4, join with sl st to first ch to form ring.

Rnd 1 (RS): Ch 2 (counts as hdc), 9 hdc in ring, join with sl st to top of beg ch-2 —10 hdc.

Rnd 2: Ch 3, 2 dc in next st, *ch 2, dc in next st, 2 dc in next st; rep from * 3 times, ch 2, join with sl st to top of beg ch-2—15 dc, 5 ch-2 sp.

Rnd 3: Ch 1, sc in first st, sc in next 2 dc, *3 sc in next ch-2 sp, sc in each of next 3 dc; rep from * 3 times, 3 sc in next ch-2 sp, cut yarn and needle-join to first st of rnd—30 sc.

Rnd 4: With D or desired red, draw up lp in any st of Rnd 3, sl st in each st around, adjusting length of sts to go nicely around the curve, cut yarn and needle-join to first st of rnd—30 sl st.

LETTUCE

With E, ch 8.

Row 1: Sc in 3rd ch from hook (creates a ch-2 lp), sc in next ch, hdc in each of next 3 ch, dc in last ch, turn—6 sts.

Row 2: Ch 1, sk first st, (sl st, ch 2, hdc) in next dc, dc in each of next 3 sts, 2 dc in last sc, 5 dc in ch-2 lp at end of row, working across opposite side of foundation ch, 2 dc in next ch, dc in each of next 3 ch, 2 hdc in next ch, one ch remains unworked, turn—19 sts.

Row 3: Ch 1, (sc, ch 2, sc) in first hdc, (hdc, ch 2, hdc) in each of next 6 sts, (hdc, ch 2, hdc) in each of next 5 sts, (hdc, ch 2, hdc) in each of next 6 sts, (sc, ch 2, sc) in top of turning ch—43 sts, 24 ch-2 sp. Fasten off E.

CHEESE SLICE (MAKE 2)

With F, ch 4, join with sl st to first ch to form ring.

Rnd 1 (RS): Ch 2 (counts as first hdc here and throughout), hdc in ring, ch 2, *2 hdc in ring, ch 2; rep from * twice, join with sl st to top of beg ch-2—8 hdc, 4 ch-2 sps.

Rnd 2: Ch 2, hdc in next st, *(hdc, ch 2, hdc) in next ch-2 sp, hdc in each of next 2 hdc; rep from * twice, (hdc, ch 2, hdc) in ch-2 sp, join with sl st to top of beg ch-2—16 hdc, 4 ch-2 sp.

Rnd 3: Ch 3 (counts as dc), dc in next 2 sts, *(2 dc, ch 2, 2 dc) in next ch-2 sp, dc in each of next 4 hdc; rep from * twice, (2 dc, ch 2, 2 dc) in next ch-2 sp, dc in next hdc, join with sl st to top of beg ch-3—32 dc, 4 ch-2 sp. Fasten off F.

ONION SLICE (MAKE 2)

With G, ch 4, join with sl st to first ch to form ring.

Rnd 1 (RS): Ch 2 (counts as hdc), 9 hdc in ring, join with sl st to top of beg ch-2 —10 hdc.

Rnd 2: Ch 1, working in BLO, 2 sc in each of next 10 sts, join with sl st in first sc of rnd—20 sc.

Rnd 3: Ch 1, working in BLO, *sc in next 3 sts, 2 sc in next st; rep from * 4 times, cut yarn and needle join to first sc of rnd—25 sc.

FINISHING

Weave in ends. Block tomato, cheese, and onion. The lettuce is supposed to be wavy.

A child will enjoy fixing you a delicious pretend sandwich for lunch, if you leave the pieces separate.

If you prefer to keep the sandwich together, stack components as desired, use a length of A to tack the layers together at 3 or 4 points.

storybook mushroom

Fly agaric mushrooms remind me of
European forests, where a gingerbread
house or enchanted hart may lurk beyond
the next tree. If you see a fly agaric in
real life, don't eat it.

SKILL LEVEL
Intermediate

MATERIALS & TOOLS
2 colors of yarn: Red (A), white or
cream (B)

Crochet hook: Appropriate size
hook to achieve a firm gauge with
selected yarn

Optional: White buttons, felt circles,
embroidery, or beads for spots

PATTERN NOTES
Read about free lps and tambour
st on pages 9 and 11. You can
substitute buttons, felt circles, or
embroidery for crocheted spots.

ABBREVIATIONS
Find instructions on page 16 for: htr

INSTRUCTIONS

LARGE MUSHROOM

Cap

With A, ch 4, join with sl st to first ch to form ring.

Row 1: Ch 3 (counts as dc here and throughout), [dc, 2 hdc, sc, 2 hdc, 2 dc] in ring, do not join, turn—9 sts.

Row 2: Ch 3, dc in first st, hdc in next st, 2 hdc in next st, hdc in each of next 3 sts, 2 hdc in next st, hdc in next st, 2 dc in next st, turn—13 sts.

Row 3: Ch 5, sl st in 2nd ch from hook (small picot made), dc2tog over first 2 sts, *hdc in next st, 2 hdc in next st; rep from * 3 times, hdc in next st, dc2tog over next st and top of turning ch, ch 2, sl st in 2nd ch from hook, ch 3, sl st in top of same turning ch—17 sts (counting ch-sts at beg and end of row as 1 st each).

Row 4: Rotate mushroom cap to work along straight edge, work 2 sl sts in the side of each of next 4 row-end sts, cut yarn and needle-join to the first ch-st of Row 3 of cap—8 sl sts.

Underside of Cap and Stem

Still working along straight edge of mushroom cap, with RS facing, draw up lp of B in first ch-st of ch-3 (after the picot) at end of Row 3, sl st in next 2 ch sts, sl st in BL of of next 4 sl sts. Begin working stem. Row will be completed later.

Make stem: ch 9;

Row 1: Hdc in 4th ch from hook, hdc in next ch, sc in each of next 4 ch, sl st in BL of next sl st of mushroom cap, turn;

Row 2: Working back along sts of Row 1, ch 1, sc in each of next 4 sc, hdc in each of next 2 hdc, hdc in turning ch of previous row, turn;

Row 3: Working toward mushroom cap, ch 3, sk first hdc, hdc in each of next 2 hdc, sc in each of next 4 sc, sl st in BL of each of next 4 sts of mushroom cap, sl st in each of next 3 ch sts. Fasten off B.

OPTIONAL SPOTS (MAKE 2 OR 3)

With B, ch 4, join with sl st to first ch to form ring.

Rnd 1: Ch 1, 7 sc in ring, leaving a long sewing length, cut yarn and needle-join to first sc of rnd.

Skirt

With B, ch 6, sl st in 2nd ch from hook, sk next ch, [hdc in next ch, ch 2, sl st in 2nd ch from hook] twice, ch 2, sl st in last ch. Fasten off, leaving a sewing length.

FINISHING

Sew 2 or 3 spots to mushroom cap, sew skirt to top of stem. Weave in ends and block.

SMALL MUSHROOM

Cap

With A, ch 6.

Row 1: Hdc in 3rd ch from hook, hdc in next ch, dc in next ch, htr in next ch, turn—4 sts, ch-2 lp.

Row 2: Ch 2, hdc in first st, hdc in each of next 2 sts, 2 hdc in next st, 2 hdc in each of next 2 ch sts, working across opposite side of foundation ch, 2 hdc in next ch, hdc in each of next 3 ch, ch 2, sl st in same ch as last st—16 sts (counting ch-sts at beg and end of row as 1 st each).

Row 3: Rotate piece to work along straight edge of mushroom cap, 3 sl st in side of htr at end of Row 1, cut yarn and needle-join to next ch-st. Fasten off A.

Stem and Spots

With RS facing, join B with a sl st in BL of last sl st of Row 2 (it will be 3rd st from end), ch 5, sl st in 2nd ch from hook (small picot made), ch 4, sl st in 2nd ch from hook (small picot made), sk 2 ch, sk base of first picot, dc in next ch, hdc in each of next 2 ch, sk next st of mushroom cap, sl st in BL of next st. Fasten off B, leaving a 12"/30cm sewing length.

Study photo to see placement and direction of spots. Take long yarn end to back of mushroom cap, insert hook from front of cap to back, about 1 st above end of stem, *draw up a lp of B, make 2 tambour sts toward side of cap, pull last lp completely out, take end to back to secure last tambour st, decide where the next spot will begin; rep from * twice or as desired, after last st is secured, weave in end and trim.

FINISHING

Weave in remaining ends; block.

> ### For Even More Fun...
> Glued to a lampshade, a set of these mushrooms would give any kid's room a storybook feel!

palm tree

I laid the small version of this tree on my outstretched hand to show my daughter, Eva. "Mom, you should put pom-poms on that!" she said. "Then it would be a pom-pom palm palm!"

For Even More Fun...
Turn your office space into an island oasis by pinning these to the fabric walls of a cubicle or placing them in small, individual frames, then hanging them on the wall. You'll feel less stressed in no time!

INSTRUCTIONS

TALL TRUNK

With A, ch 7.

Row 1: Sc in 2nd ch from hook, sc in each ch across, turn—6 sc.

Rows 2–4: Ch 1, sc in BLO of each sc across, turn—6 sc in each row.

Row 5: Ch 1, working in BLO, sc in each of first 2 sts, sc2tog over next 2 sts, sc in last 2 sts, turn—5 sts.

Rows 6–10: Ch 1, sc in BLO of each sc across, turn—5 sc.

Row 11: Ch 1, working in BLO, sc in each of first 2 sts, sc2tog over next 2 sts, sc in last st, turn—4 sc.

Rows 12–16: Ch 1, sc in BLO of each sc across, turn—4 sc.

Row 17: Ch 1, working in BLO, sc in first st, sc2tog over next 2 sts, sc in last st, turn—3 sts.

Rows 18–20: Ch 1, sc in BLO of each sc across—3 sc.

Fasten off, leaving a long sewing length.

SMALL TRUNK

With A, ch 6.

Row 1: Sc in 2nd ch from hook, sc in each ch across, turn—5 sc.

Rows 2–5: Ch 1, sc in BLO of each sc across, turn—5 sc.

Rows 6–15: Work Rows 11–20 of Tall Trunk. Fasten off, leaving a long sewing length.

FRONDS

With RS facing, join B with sl st to first st of last row of trunk, *ch 9, sl st in 4th ch from hook (for picot), ch 6, sl st in 4th ch from hook (for picot), [ch 4, sl st in 4th ch from hook] twice (2 picots); working back along picot ch you just made, sk next 3 picots, sl st in next 2 ch, ch 4, sl st in 4th ch from hook, sk next picot, sl st in each of rem 5 ch*, sl st in same st at top of trunk, [rep from * to * once, sl st into next st at top of trunk, rep from * to * once, sl st in same st at top of trunk] twice. Fasten off.

FINISHING

If you want your palm tree to stand straight, simply weave in ends. If you want your palm tree to bend, thread sewing length at top of trunk onto a tapestry needle. Weave yarn down one side of trunk and pull to gather. Tack yarn to hold bend in place. Weave in ends. Block fronds. To preserve its corrugated texture, do not block trunk.

gardening hat

While you wait for the weather to turn warm enough for planting, here's a project to remind you of the joys of gardening. In spite of all the colors, you will only have two yarn ends to weave in.

SKILL LEVEL
Easy

MATERIALS & TOOLS
3 or 4 colors of yarn as desired: Hat color (A), optional band color (B), leaf color (C), flower color (D)

Crochet hook: Appropriate size hook to achieve a firm gauge with selected yarn

Tapestry needle

Small amount of polyester fiberfill

Optional: Embroidery floss, beads, or buttons for embellishment

ABBREVIATIONS
Find instructions on page 16 for: FLO

INSTRUCTIONS

HAT WITH NO HATBAND

With A, ch 4, join with a sl st to form a ring.

Rnd 1: Ch 1, 6 sc in ring, join with sl st to first sc—6 sc.

Rnd 2: Ch 1, 2 sc in each st around, join with sl st to first sc—12 sc.

Rnd 3: Ch 1, *sc in next 3 sc, 2 sc in next sc; rep from * twice, join with sl st to first sc—15 sc.

Rnd 4: Ch 1, sc in each sc around, join with sl st to first sc.

Rnd 5: Ch 1, *2 sc in next st, sc in next 4 sts; rep from * twice, join with sl st to first sc—18 sc. Note: This rnd finishes the crown of the hat.

Rnd 6: Working in FLO, ch 1, starting in first st, *sc in each of next 2 sts, 2 sc in

next st; rep from * around, join with sl st to first sc of rnd—24 sc.

Rnd 7: Ch 1, 2 sc in first st, sc in next 3 sts, *2 sc in next st, sc in each of next 3 sts; rep from * 4 times, join with sl st to first sc—30 sc.

Rnd 8: Ch 1, starting in first st, *sc in each of next 2 sts, 2 sc in next st, sc in each of next 2 sts; rep from * around, join with sl st to first sc of rnd—36 sc.

Rnd 9: Ch 1, starting in first st, *sc in each of next 5 sts, 2 sc in next st, rep from * around, join with sl st to first sc—42 sc.

Rnd 10: Ch 1, sc in first st, ch 2, sl st in 2nd ch from hook (picot), sk next st, *sc in next st, ch 2, sl st in 2nd ch from hook (picot), sk next st; rep from * around, cut yarn and needle-join to first sc of rnd OR join with sl st to first sc of rnd and fasten off—21 sc alternating with 21 small picots.

HAT WITH HATBAND

Work same as Hat with No Hatband through Rnd 4. At the end of Rnd 4, open the last lp wide and thread the ball of (A) through it. Tighten thread, but do not cut yarn.

Rnd 5: Join B with a sc in any st of Rnd 4, sc in same st, *sc in each of next 4 sts, 2 sc in next st; rep from * once, sc in each of next 4 sts, join with sl st to first sc of rnd—18 sc. Fasten off B. This rnd finishes the crown of the hat.

Rnd 6: Pick up A, and working this rnd in FLO, sl st in nearest st of Rnd 5, ch 1, sc in same st as sl st, sc in next st, 2 sc in next st, *sc in next 2 sts, 2 sc in next st; rep from * 4 times around, join with sl st to first sc—24 sc.

Rnds 7–10: Work same as Rnds 7–10 as for Hat with No Hatband.

FOR THESE HATS WE USED

Classic Elite Yarns Woodland (65% wool, 35% nettles; 1¾oz/50g = 131yd/100m) DK weight yarn (3): #3150 Sunshine (A), #3154 Red Grape (B), #3168 Deep Salmon (D); Mill Hill seed and bugle beads.

GAUGE CIRCLE
(see page 7) = 1"/2.5cm worked on 4.00mm (size G-6 U.S.) hook

FINISHED MEASUREMENT
3"/7.6cm in diameter

Classic Elite Yarns Liberty Wool (100% washable wool; 1¾oz/50g = 122yd/111m) DK weight yarn (3): #7880 Golden Poppy (A), #7894 Jade (C), #7858 Scarlet (D).

GAUGE CIRCLE
(see page 7) = ⅞"/2.2cm worked on 4.00mm (size G-6 U.S.) hook

FINISHED MEASUREMENT
2¾"/7cm in diameter

Berroco Captiva (60% cotton, 23% polyester, 17% acrylic; 1.75oz/50g = 98yd/90m) medium weight yarn (4): #5520 Honey (A), #5530 Marina (B); Anchor embroidery floss in red and green.

GAUGE CIRCLE
(see page 7) = almost 1"/2.5cm worked on 4.00mm (size G-6 U.S.) hook

FINISHED MEASUREMENT
3¼"/8.3cm in diameter

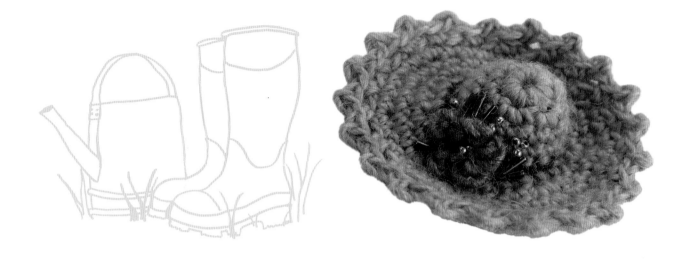

Inside Cover for Crown of Hat

With A, ch 5, join with sl st to first ch to form ring.

Rnd 1: Ch 2 (counts as hdc), 8 hdc in ring, join with sl st to top of beg ch-2. Fasten off, leaving a sewing length—9 hdc.

Leaves

With C, leaving a 4"/10cm sewing length, *ch 4, sl st in 2nd, 3rd, and 4th ch from hook*, ch 2, rep from * to *. Fasten off, leaving a 4"/10cm sewing length.

Flower

With D, leaving a 4"/10cm sewing length, wrap yarn around your finger to create a lp, insert hook into thread lp and draw up a lp, [ch 3, sl st into thread lp] 5 times. Fasten off, leaving 4"/10cm sewing length, pull first yarn end to tighten lp and close the center of the flower.

FINISHING

Weave in the yarn end at the brim of the hat only.

To embellish with crocheted flowers and leaves, from inside of the hat, insert hook between any 2 sts of Rnd 5, hook one yarn end of leaves and pull the end into crown. Skip 2 sts of Rnd 5, insert hook, and pull in other yarn end of leaves. From inside of hat, insert hook between 2 leaf yarn ends and insert it into ch-2 between the 2 leaves, hook both yarn ends of flower, pull ends through to inside of hat's crown. Holding leaf yarn ends in one hand and flower yarn ends in other hand, tie two pairs together in a square knot. Stuff ends into crown of hat.

Alternatively, embroider French knot flowers and ch-st leaves on hat or sew beads to hat to represent flowers and leaves.

Find line of lps on inside of hat's crown, formed by working in FLO of Rnd 6. Using sewing length, sew each st of inside cover for crown of hat to every other lp inside crown, stuffing other yarn ends into crown and adding fiberfill if necessary to lightly fill crown.

Block brim of hat.

vintage grapes

Jelly made from native Texas mustang grapes is a taste of summer in a jar. Its fancy greenery inspired these leaves. Old-fashioned padded crochet, or bullion stitch, grapes complete the design.

FOR THESE GRAPE CLUSTERS WE USED

Berroco Ultra® Alpaca Light (50% super fine alpaca, 50% Peruvian wool; 1.75oz/50g = 144yd/133m) sport weight yarn (**2**): #4275 Pea Soup Mix (A), #4283 Lavender Mix (B).

GAUGE CIRCLE
(see page 7) = ⅞"/2.2cm worked on 3.75mm (size F-5 U.S.) hook

FINISHED MEASUREMENT
4"/10.2cm x 3¾"/9.5cm for the leaf, excluding stem; 1"/2.5cm for a bullion grape

Classic Elite Yarns Majestic Tweed (40% wool, 20% angora, 20% silk, 20% nylon; 1¾oz/50g = 110yd/119m) worsted weight yarn (**4**): #7235 Olive (A), #7227 Cognac (B).

GAUGE CIRCLE
(see page 7) = 1³⁄₁₆"/3cm worked on 5.00mm (size H-8 U.S.) hook

FINISHED MEASUREMENT
5¼"/13.3cm x 5⅛"/13cm for the leaf, excluding stem; 1¼"/3.2cm for a single Padded Grape

INSTRUCTIONS

GRAPE LEAF

With A, ch 5, join with sl st to form ring.

Rnd 1: Ch 3 (counts as dc), 11 dc in ring, join with sl st to top of beg ch-3—12 dc.

Rnd 2:

Lobe 1: Ch 6, working back toward center along ch, dc in 4th ch from hook, dc in each of next 2 ch, sk 1 st of Rnd 1, sl st in next st—3 dc, 3 ch, 3 free lps;

Lobe 2: Ch 8, working back toward center along ch, dc in 4th ch from hook, dc in each of next 4 ch, sk 1 st of Rnd 1, sl st in next st—5 dc, 3 ch, 5 free lps;

Lobe 3: Ch 10, working back toward center along ch, dc in 4th ch from hook, dc in each of next 6 ch, sk 1 st of Rnd 1, sl st in next st—7 dc, 3 ch, 7 free lps;

Lobe 4: Ch 8, working back toward center along ch, dc in 4th ch from hook, dc in each of next 4 ch, sk 1 st of Rnd 1, sl st in next st—5 dc, 3 ch, 5 free lps;

Lobe 5: Ch 6, working back toward center along ch, dc in 4th ch from hook, dc in each of next 2 ch, sk 1 st of Rnd 1, sl st in next st—3 dc, 3 ch, 3 free lps.

Rnd 3: Ch 2,

Lobe 1: Sc in first free lp, sc-picot, sk next free lp, sl st in next free lp, make point as follows: (ch 4, sc in 3rd ch from hook, hdc in next st), sl st in 2nd ch of ch-3 lp, sc-picot, sk next ch, sc in each of next 2 dc, draw up a lp in next dc, draw up a lp in sl st bet lobes, draw up a lp in first free lp of next lobe, yo and draw through all lps on hook (sc3tog made)—2 picots, 1 point;

Lobe 2: Sc in each of next 2 free lps, hdc in next free lp, make point as follows: (ch

5, sl st in 3rd ch from hook, sc in next ch, hdc in next ch), sl st in same free lp as hdc before point, make next point as follows: (ch 7, sl st in 3rd ch from hook, sc in next ch, hdc in next ch, dc in next ch, htr in next ch), skip next ch-3 at end of lobe, sl st in next dc, sc-picot, sc in next dc, sk next dc, dc3tog placing sts in next dc, first free lp of Lobe 3, and 3rd free lp of Lobe 3—1 picot, 2 points;

Lobe 3: Dc in each of next 2 free lps, make point as follows: (ch 5, sl st in 3rd ch from hook, sc in next ch, [hdc, dc] in next ch), sl st in same free lp as dc before point, sc in next 2 free lps, make small point as follows: (ch 4, sl st in 3rd ch from hook, sc in next ch), sl st in same free lp as sc before small point, make top point as follows: (ch 7, sl st in 3rd ch from hook, sc in next ch, hdc in next ch, dc in next ch, htr in next ch), sk next ch-3 at end of

lobe, sl st in next dc, make small point as follows: (ch 4, sl st in 3rd ch from hook, sc in next ch), sc in same dc as sl st before small point, sc in next dc, sl st in next dc, make point as follows: (ch 6, sl st in 3rd ch from hook, sc in next ch, hdc-dc-tog over next 2 ch), dc in same st as sl st before point, dc in next st, dc3tog placing sts in next dc, last dc of lobe, and 2nd free lp of Lobe 4—5 points;

Lobe 4: Sk next free lp, sc in next free lp, sc-picot, sl st in next free lp, make point as follows: (ch 7, sl st in 3rd ch from hook, working down chain, sc in next ch, hdc in next ch, dc in next ch, htr in next ch), sk next ch-3 at end of lobe, sl st in next dc, make point as follows: (ch 5, sl st in 3rd ch from hook, sc in next ch, hdc in next ch), hdc in same dc as sl st before point, hdc in next dc, sc in next 2 dc, draw up a lp in next dc, draw up a lp in sl st bet lobes,

draw up a lp in first free lp of next lobe, yo and draw through all lps on hook (sc3tog made)—1 picot, 2 points;

Lobe 5: Sc in next 2 free lps, sc-picot, sk 1 ch, sl st in next ch, make point as follows: (ch 4, sc in 3rd ch from hook, hdc in next st), sk next ch-st, sl st in next dc, sc-picot, sk next dc, sc in last dc of lobe—2 picots, 1 point.

To make a stem, follow instructions below, otherwise, sl st into ch-2 sp and fasten off.

Stem (optional)

Sl st in first ch of ch-2 sp, ch 16 or desired length of stem, sc in 3rd ch from hook, sl st in each ch across; cut yarn and needle-join to 2nd ch of ch-2 space OR sl st in 2nd ch of ch-2 space and fasten off yarn.

PADDED GRAPES (MAKE 9 OR MORE)

With B, ch 5, join with sl st to form ring.

Rnd 1 (RS): Ch 1, 12 sc (or more) in ring, join with sl st to first st of rnd.

Rnd 2: Working over sts in Rnd 1, work at least 12 sc in center ring, covering Rnd 1 as you go; leaving a long sewing length, cut yarn and needle-join to first st of rnd OR join with sl st to first sc of rnd and, leaving a long sewing length, fasten off yarn. To give padded grapes more dimension, pinch outer edge of sts toward WS of piece.

BULLION GRAPES (MAKE 8 OR MORE)

Ch 4, join with sl st in first ch to form a ring.

Rnd 1: Ch 1, 8 sc in ring, join with sl st in first sc—8 sc.

Rnd 2: Ch 1, *7 wraps around hook, insert hook into center of ring, yo and pull lp through center and all wraps on hook (bullion st complete), ch 1 to secure bullion st; rep from * 6 times, join with sl st in first sc—7 bullion sts; leaving a long sewing length, cut yarn and needle-join to first st of rnd OR fasten off yarn—18 sc.

Tendril

With A, ch 60 or desired length; sl st in 2nd ch from hook, *sk 1 ch, sl st in next st; rep from * across to end of ch. Fasten off A, leaving a long sewing length. Arrange tendril into a coil.

FINISHING

Leaf: Weave in ends and block, taking time to unfurl points and pin them if necessary.

Grapes: Weave in end at beg of each grape. Arrange grapes as desired to make a bunch, use sewing lengths to sew grapes together, weave in ends before trimming yarn.

Sew leaf to grape bunch. Use sewing length to sew tendril in place, weave in rem ends.

flower basket

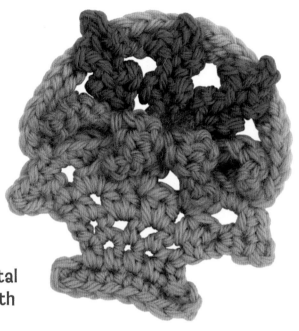

I love folk art stencils and paintings of flowers in a pedestal basket or vase. Those, along with a friend's basket-motif quilts, inspired this design.

SKILL LEVEL
Intermediate

MATERIALS & TOOLS
3 colors of yarn: Basket color (A), greenery color (B), flower color (C)

Crochet hook: Appropriate size hook to achieve a firm gauge with selected yarn

Tapestry needle

Optional: Sewing thread and needle

ABBREVIATIONS
Find instructions on page 16 for: BL

INSTRUCTIONS

BASKET

With A, ch 8.

Row 1 (RS): Sc in 3rd ch from hook, sc in each of next 5 ch, ch 3, rotate piece to work across opposite side of foundation ch, sl st in first ch—6 sc.

Row 2 (also RS): Ch 2 (counts as first hdc), hdc in each of next 4 ch, turn—5 hdc.

Row 3: Ch 3 (counts as hdc, ch 1), *hdc in next st, ch 1; rep from * twice, hdc in top of turning ch from previous row, turn—5 hdc separated by ch-1 sps.

Row 4: Ch 2 (counts as hdc here and throughout), hdc in next ch-1 sp, *ch 1, 2 hdc in next ch-1 sp; rep from * once, ch 1, hdc in next ch-sp, hdc in 2nd ch of turning ch, turn—8 hdc, 3 ch-1 sp.

Row 5: Ch 2, hdc in first st, *ch 2, 2 hdc in next ch-1 sp; rep from * twice, ch 2, 2 hdc in top of beg ch-2, turn—5 pairs of hdc separated by ch-2 sps.

Row 6 (RS): Ch 3, *sc in each of next 2 hdc, 2 sc in next ch-2 sp; rep from * 3 times, sc in next hdc, (sc, ch 2, sl st) in top of beg ch-2—18 sc. Fasten off yarn.

LEAVES

With RS of basket facing, join B with a sl st in BL of 5th sc of Row 6, *ch 6, sl st in 3rd ch from hook, working down ch toward basket, sc in next ch, hdc in next ch, dc in

next ch, sk next sc in Row 5, sl st in BL of next st; rep from * 3 times. Fasten off B.

FLOWERS

Bend leaves to front and out of way, join C with a sl st in BL of skipped st under first leaf, with C draw up lp, *ch 2, slst-picot, ch 1, (slst-picot) 3 times for top of flower, working back down toward basket, sk next 3 picots, sl st in next ch st, slst-picot, sk next picot, sl st in each of next 2 ch, sl st in BL of skipped st behind next leaf; rep from * twice. Fasten off C.

HANDLE

With RS facing, join A with a sl st in 3rd sc of Row 6, ch 1, sc in same st, *draw up lp in side of sc just completed, yo, draw through both lps on hook; rep from * 25 times or desired length of handle. Fasten off A leaving a sewing length. Sew handle end to 3rd from last st of Row 6.

FINISHING

Weave in ends. Block basket and flowers. If desired, let leaves curl out over edge of basket, otherwise block them, too. For added stability (especially of handle), with sewing thread, sew flowers and (some) leaves to each other and to basket handle.

seashell

While most of the scallops we see in restaurants are just a couple of inches in diameter, some types of scallops can grow up to nine inches! These scallop shells are a bit smaller—use them to embellish towels in a beach house or a guest bathroom.

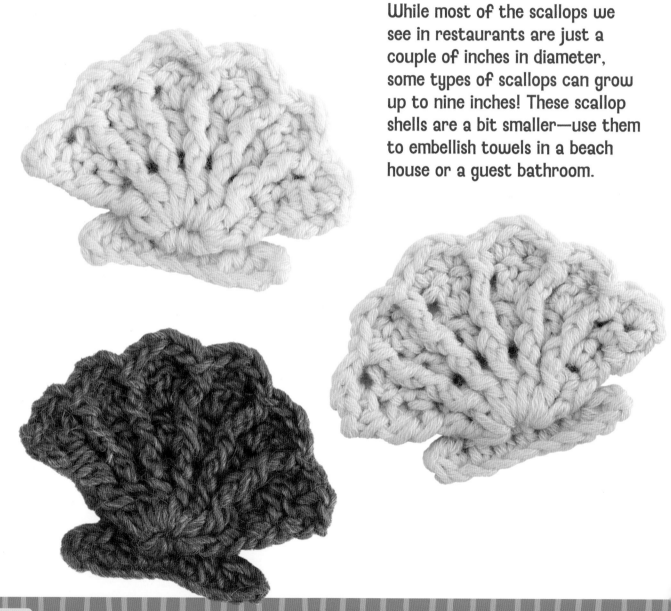

INSTRUCTIONS

SHELL

With A, leaving a long sewing length, ch 5, join with sl st to form ring.

Rnd 1 (RS): Ch 3 (counts as dc), 11 dc in ring, join with sl st to top of beg ch-3, turn—12 sts.

Work now progresses in rows.

Row 2 (WS): Ch 2 (counts as hdc here and throughout), BPhdc in next st, ch 1, (BPdc in next st, ch 1) 5 times, BPhdc in next st, hdc in next st, turn—9 sts and 6 ch. Some sts of Rnd 1 remain unworked.

Row 3 (RS): Ch 2, FPhdc around next st, hdc in next ch-1 sp, [FPdc around next st, dc in next ch-1 sp] 4 times, FPdc around next st, hdc in next ch-1 sp, FPhdc around next st, hdc in top of turning ch, turn—15 sts.

Row 4 (WS): Ch 2, BPhdc around next st, 2 hdc in next st, BPhdc around next st, *2 dc in next st, BPdc around next st; rep from * twice, 2 dc in next st, BPhdc around next st, 2 hdc in next st, BPhdc around next st, hdc in top of turning ch, turn—21 sts.

Row 5 (RS): Ch 1, sc in first st, FPsc around first rib st, [(sc, hdc) in next st, sc in next st, FPsc around next rib st] twice, [(sc, hdc) in next dc, (hdc, sc) in next dc, FPsc around next rib st] twice, [(sc, hdc) in next st, sc in next st, FPsc around next rib st] twice, sc in top of turning ch—a border of 6 small shells separated by post sts. Fasten off, leaving a long sewing length.

SHELL FOOT

With A, leaving a long sewing length, ch 10.

Row 1: Sc in 2nd ch from hook, hdc in next ch, dc in each of next 5 ch, hdc in next ch, (sc, ch 1, sl st) in last ch. Fasten off.

FINISHING

Fold unworked sts of Rnd 1 to back of shell and sew in place with long yarn end. Fold under sts running up each side of shell and hem in place, so that rib formed by post-sts is at edge.

Center base of shell on foot using photo as a guide for placement, sew in place. Weave in remaining ends, block.

horse chestnut leaf

Whacking horse chestnuts is an important skill we learned while living in England. This pattern, for the horse chestnut tree's striking leaves, is easy to conker. No, that wasn't a typo.

SKILL LEVEL
Intermediate

MATERIALS & TOOLS
1 color of yarn: Leaf color (A)

Crochet hook: Appropriate size hook to achieve a firm gauge with selected yarn

Tapestry needle

Embroidery floss, beads, or buttons to decorate center of flower

ABBREVIATIONS
Find instructions on pages 16 and 17 for: htr, st-top-picot

FOR THESE LEAVES WE USED

Classic Elite Yarns Liberty Wool (100% washable wool; 1¾oz/50g = 122yd/111m) DK/sport weight yarn (3): #7835 Citronella, #7850 Gold, #7880 Golden Poppy, or #7818 Fresh Clay (A).

GAUGE CIRCLE
(see page 7) = ⅞"/2.2cm worked on 4.00mm (size G-6 U.S.) hook

FINISHED MEASUREMENT
3¾"/9.5cm x 4¾"/12.1cm, including stem

INSTRUCTIONS

CHESTNUT LEAF

Row 1: With A,

Lobe 1: Ch 9, sl st in 6th ch from hook, ch 2, sk next 2 ch, sl st in next st—1 ch-2 sp, 1 ch-5 lp;

Lobe 2: Ch 12, sl st in 6th ch from hook, [ch 2, sk next 2 sts, sl st in next st] twice—2 ch-2 sps, 1 ch-5 lp;

Lobe 3: Ch 15, sl st in 6th ch from hook, [ch 2, sk 2 sts, sl st in next st] 3 times—3 ch-2 sps, 1 ch-5 lp;

Lobe 4: Work same as Lobe 2;

Lobe 5: Work same as Lobe 1, turn.

Row 2:
Lobe 5: (Sl st, sc) in next ch-2 sp, (hdc, 2 dc, 2 htr, st-top-picot, 2 htr, 2 dc, hdc) in next ch-5 lp, working down other side of lobe, (sc, sl st) in next ch-2 sp, rotate piece so you are looking at the base of the lobe, sl st around the sl st at base of lobe, rotate piece to work up side of next lobe.

Lobe 4: Sl st in first ch-2 sp, (sl st, sc, hdc) in 2nd ch-2 sp, (2 dc, 2 htr, tr, st-top-picot, tr, 2 htr, 2 dc) in next ch-5 lp, working down other side of lobe, (hdc, sc, sl st) in next ch-2 sp, sl st in last ch-2 sp, rotate piece so you are looking at the base of the lobe, sl st around the sl st at base of lobe, rotate piece to work up side of next lobe.

Lobe 3: Sl st in first ch-2 sp, (sl st, sc) in 2nd ch-2 sp, (2 hdc, dc) in 3rd ch-2 sp, (3 htr, 2 tr, st-top-picot, 2 tr, 3 htr) in next ch-5 lp, working down other side of lobe, (dc, 2 hdc) in next ch-2 sp, (sc, sl st) in next ch-2 sp, sl st in last ch-2 sp, rotate piece so you are looking at the base of the lobe, sl st around the sl st at base of lobe, rotate piece to work up side of next lobe.

Lobe 2: Work same as Lobe 4.

Lobe 1: (Sl st, sc) in next ch-2 sp, (hdc, 2 dc, 2 htr, st-top-picot, 2 htr, 2 dc, hdc) in next ch-5 lp, working down other side of

lobe, (sc, sl st) in next ch-2 sp, rotate piece so you are looking at the base of the lobe, sl st around the sl st at base of lobe, rotate piece to work along the base of the lobes.

Row 3: Skip Lobe 1, [yo, draw up a lp in next lobe, yo, draw through 2 lps on hook] 3 times, draw up a lp in base of Lobe 5, yo and draw through all lps on hook.

Stem

Ch 16 or desired length of stem, sc in 3rd ch from hook, sl st in each ch across, join with sl st to base of Lobe 5 and fasten off OR cut yarn and needle-join to the base of Lobe 5.

FINISHING

Weave in ends and block.

cherry blossom

Pink, flowery trees are a lovely springtime treat. Vary the blossoms by working tree-top rounds in different colors. Or branch out and use variegated pinks or even ... green!

SKILL LEVEL
Easy

MATERIALS & TOOLS
2 or more colors of yarn as desired: Trunk color (A), medium cherry blossom color (B), optional light blossom color (C), darker blossom color (D)

Crochet hook: Appropriate size hook to achieve a firm gauge with selected yarn

Tapestry needle

Optional: Beads or buttons to embellish tree, with sewing needle and thread

PATTERN NOTE
To join branch tips with hdc: Yo, insert hook in ch-2 lp at tip of branch, insert hook in appropriate st of cherry blossom piece, draw up a lp through the st and the branch tip, yo, draw through all 3 lps on hook.

FOR THESE TREES WE USED
Dale of Norway Falk (100% superwash wool; 1¾oz/50g = 116yd/106m) DK weight yarn (3): #3072 Cocoa (A), #4415 Pink (B), #0017 Off-White (C), #4516 Peony (D).

GAUGE CIRCLE
(see page 7) = 1"/2.5cm worked on 4.00mm (size G-6 U.S.) hook

FINISHED MEASUREMENT
2½"/6.4cm x 4¼"/10.8cm

Coats & Clark Aunt Lydia's Classic Crochet Thread, No. 10, Art. 154 (100% mercerized cotton, 350yd/320m solid colors; 300yd/273m shaded colors) 10-count crochet thread (0): #21 Linen (A), #15 Shaded Pinks or #397 Wasabi (B).

GAUGE CIRCLE
(see page 7) = ⅜"/9mm worked on 2.00mm (size 4 steel U.S.) hook

FINISHED MEASUREMENT
1¼"/3.2cm x 2¼"/5.7cm

INSTRUCTIONS

TRUNK

With A, ch 14.

Branch 1

Ch 7, sl st in 3rd ch from hook (this creates a ch-2 lp at the tip of the branch), sl st in next 4 ch.

Branch 2

Ch 8, sl st in 3rd ch from hook, sl st in next st.

Branch 3

Ch 6, sl st in 3rd ch from hook, sl st in next 3 ch, sk the space created by branch 2, sl st in next 4 ch.

Working across remaining ch-sts, sc in each of next 4 ch, sk next ch, hdc in each of next 6 ch, dc in each of next 3 ch. Fasten off A.

SOLID-COLOR CHERRY BLOSSOMS

With B, ch 5, sl st in first ch-st to form ring.

Rnd 1: Ch 2 (counts as first hdc), 9 hdc in ring, sl st to top of beg ch-2—10 hdc.

Rnd 2: Ch 2 (counts as hdc here and throughout), hdc in first st, 2 hdc in next 9 hdc, join with sl st to top of beg ch-2 —20 hdc.

Rnd 3: Ch 2, hdc in next st, join the tip of branch 1 with hdc in the same st (see Pattern Notes), [hdc in next st, 2 hdc in next st] 3 times, hdc in next st, join tip of branch 2 with hdc in next st, hdc in same st, [hdc in next st, 2 hdc in next st] 5 times, join with sl st to top of beg ch-2—30 hdc.

Rnd 4: Sk next hdc, *5 hdc in next st (shell made), sk next st, sl st in next st, sk next st; rep from * twice, 5 hdc in next st, sk next st, insert hook in ch-2 lp at tip of branch 3, insert hook in next st of Rnd 3, yo and draw through all lps on hook (sl st join made), sk next st, 5 hdc in next st, sk next st, sl st in next st—5 shells. Fasten off, leaving a sewing length, leaving rem sts unworked. This is a partial rnd.

THREE-COLOR CHERRY BLOSSOMS

Work same as for Solid-Color Cherry Blossoms in the following color sequence:

Center Rnd and Rnd 1: C.

Rnds 2 and 3: B.

Rnd 4: D.

FINISHING

Weave the long end of B or D through the back of the cherry blossom piece about 3 sts beyond the end of Rnd 4, use end to tack the tree trunk to the edge of the cherry blossom piece.

Weave in ends. Block. Embellish with beads or buttons as desired.

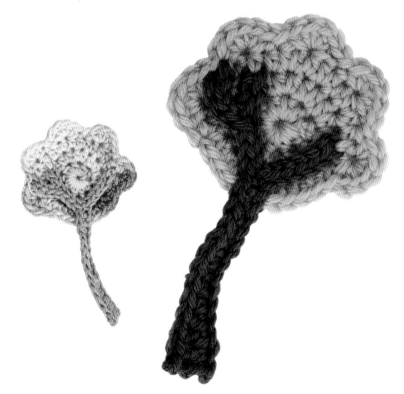

umbrella

April showers bring May flowers, it's said. In our region of Texas, good winter rains guarantee flowers from March through June! Whenever your flower-bringing showers happen, stay dry inside while you crochet this bright umbrella.

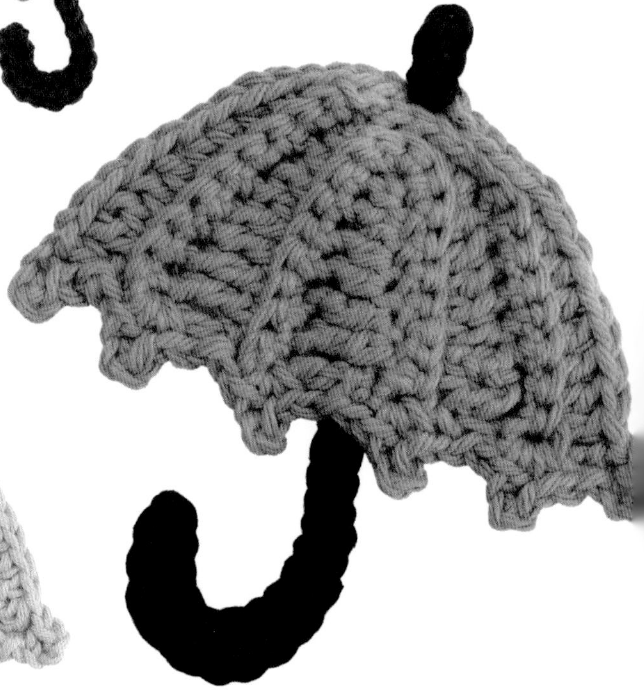

SKILL LEVEL
Intermediate

MATERIALS & TOOLS
2 colors of yarn: Umbrella color (A), handle color (B)

Crochet hook: Appropriate size hook to achieve a firm gauge with selected yarn

Tapestry needle

ABBREVIATIONS
Find instructions on pages 16 and 17 for: BLO, htr, joined-tr, RS, slst-picot, WS

INSTRUCTIONS

UMBRELLA
Using With A, ch 9.

Row 1 (RS): Sc in 3rd ch from hook (this creates a ch-2 loop which that is at top of umbrella), working along the ch, hdc in each of next 2 ch, dc in next ch, htr in next ch, tr in each of last 2 ch, turn—(7 sts.)

Row 2 (WS): Ch 1, working in BLO, sc in each of the first 2 tr, 2 sc in next htr, sc in each of the last 4 sts; 3 sc in ch-2 loop at top of umbrella; rotate the piece to work in the opposite side of foundation ch, sc in each of next 4 ch, 2 sc in next ch (at the base of the htr of Rrow 1), sc in each of last 2 ch, turn—(19 sc.)

Row 3 (RS): Ch 4 (counts as tr), working in BLO, joined-tr in next sc, tr in next st, htr in next st, 2 dc in next st, dc in next st, hdc in next st, sc in next st, ch 1; sl st in each of 3 sts at top of umbrella; rotate piece to work along its other side, ch 1, sc in next st, hdc in next st, dc in next st, 2 dc in next st, htr in next st, tr in each or last 3 sts, turn—(23 sts.)

Row 4 (WS): Ch 1, working in BLO, sc in each of first 9 sts, ch 1, sl st in next ch, sl st in each of next 3 sts at top of umbrella, sl st in next ch, ch 1, sc in each of next 8 sts, sc in top of ch-4 turning ch, turn—(25 sts.)

Row 5 (RS): Ch 3 (counts as dc), working in BLO, 2 dc in next st, dc in each of next 2

sts, hdc each of in next 3 sts, sc in next st, ch 1, sl st in next sc, sl st in next ch, sl st in each of next 2 sl-sts, ch 2, sk next st which is at top of umbrella, sl st in each of next 2 sl sts, sl st in next ch, sl st in next sc, ch 1, sc in next st, hdc in each of next 3 sts, dc in each of next 2 sts, 2 dc in next st, dc in last sc.

Rotate piece to work points along the lower edge of the umbrella:

Ch 1, slst-picot, ch 1, sl st in the side of the last dc of Row 5, ch 1, *(sc, slst-picot, sc) in the side of the next sc, ch 1, sl st in the side of the next tr, ch 1; rep from * once, (sc, slst-picot, sc) in the side of the next sc, ch 1, sl st in the turning ch at the beg of Row 3, ch 1, (sc, slst-picot, sc) in the side of the next sc, ch 1, sl st in the turning ch at the beg of Row 5, ch 1, slst-picot, ch 1, sl st or needle-join to the top of the next dc of Row 5. Fasten off.

Point and Handle

With B, ch 5, sl st in 3rd ch from hook (this creates a ch-2 loop), sl st in rem 2 sts (Point made);

For the Handle, ch 27, sc in 3rd and 4th ch from hook, [2 sc in next st, sc in next st] twice, sc in each of next 2 ch, sl st in each rem ch across. Fasten off, leaving a long sewing length.

FINISHING

Weave in ends of umbrella. Insert crochet hook from front to back through the ch-2 sp in Row 5 at the top of the umbrella, insert hook into ch-2 loop at end of Point, pull Point through stopping before yarn ends emerge. Use one yarn end to sew the point in place from the back. Use the other yarn end to tack the stem of the Handle down the middle of the wrong side of the umbrella. Weave in rem ends. Leave the hooked part of the handle free.

FOR THESE UMBRELLAS WE USED

Lion Brand Sock-Ease™ (75% wool, 25% nylon; 3.5oz/100g = 438yd/400m) super fine weight yarn (**1**): #206 Sour Ball (A), #200 Toffee (B).

GAUGE CIRCLE
(see page 7) = $^{11}/_{16}$"/1.7cm worked on 3.25mm (size 0 steel U.S.) hook

FINISHED MEASUREMENT
2¾"/7cm across

Lion Brand LB Collection Cotton Bamboo (52% cotton, 48% rayon from bamboo; 3.5oz/100g = 245yd/224m) light weight yarn (**3**): #170 Gardenia (A), #126 Chocolate Dahlia (B).

GAUGE CIRCLE
(see page 7) = 1"/2.5cm worked on 4.00mm (size G-6 U.S.) hook

FINISHED MEASUREMENT
3⅞"/9.8cm across

Lion Brand Kitchen Cotton (100% cotton; 2oz/57g = 99yd/90m) medium weight yarn (**4**): #103 Bubblegum (A), #153 Licorice (B).

GAUGE CIRCLE
(see page 7) = 1¼"/3.2cm worked on 5.00mm (size H-8 U.S.) hook

FINISHED MEASUREMENT
5⅛"/13cm across

gingerbread kids

Make a family of gingerbread people by using bigger yarn and hooks for larger folk. Whatever you do, keep them away from foxes!

SKILL LEVEL
Easy

MATERIALS & TOOLS
2 colors of yarn: Gingerbread color (A), icing color (B)

Crochet hook: Appropriate size hook to achieve a firm gauge with selected yarn

Tapestry needle

Optional: Embroidery floss, beads, or buttons to add features, with sewing needle and thread

PATTERN NOTES
Read about crocheting into free lps on page 9. After you make multiple sts into ch-lps at ends of arms and legs in Rnd 2, the initial st after the ch-lp is usually obscured, so I ask you to skip that st. Most likely, you won't be able to see it anyway. To orient yourself, count remaining sts, compare to instructions, and make sure they will work out correctly.

ABBREVIATIONS
Find instructions on pages 16 and 17 for: sc2tog, hdc2tog

INSTRUCTIONS

GINGERBREAD BOY

Rnd 1: With A,

First arm

Ch 8, sc in 3rd ch from hook, sc in each of next 5 ch—6 sc, 6 free lps, ch-2 lp at end of arm;

Head

Ch 8, hdc in 3rd ch from hook, sc in next 5 sts—6 sts, 6 free lps, ch-2 lp at top of head;

Second arm

Ch 8, sc in 3rd ch from hook, sc in each of next 4 ch, draw up a lp in next ch, draw up lp in side of sc at base of head, yo, draw up lp in side of sc at base of first arm, yo, draw through all lps on hook (2sc-hdc-tog made)—6 sts, 6 free lps, ch-2 lp at end of arm;

Body and first leg

Ch 11, sc in 3rd ch from hook, sc in each of next 4 ch-sts, sc2tog over next 2 ch, 2 ch rem unworked—6 sts, 7 free lps, ch-2 lp at end of leg;

Second leg and body

Ch 8, sc in 3rd ch from hook, sc in each of next 4 sts, 2 sc in next ch, draw up lp in side of sc at base of first leg, draw up lp in next ch, yo, draw through all lps on hook (sc2tog made), hdc in next ch to complete body—7 sts, 6 free lps, ch-2 lp at end, 2 sts and free lps for body.

Rnd 2:
First arm

Working across opposite side of foundation ch of first arm, sc in each of next 6 ch, 5 sc in next ch-2 lp at end of arm, sk next sc, sc in each of next 3 sts, sc2tog over next 2 sts;

Head

Working across opposite side of foundation ch of head, sk first 2 ch, sc2tog over next 2 ch, hdc in next ch, dc in next ch, 8 dc in next ch-2 lp at top of head, sk next hdc, dc in next st, hdc in next st, sc2tog over next 2 sts, sk next st;

Second arm

Working across opposite side of foundation ch of second arm, sc2tog over first 2 ch, sc in each of next 4 ch, 5 sc in next ch-2 lp at end of arm, sk next sc, sc in each of next 4 sts, sc-hdc-tog over next st and first free lp of body;

Body and first leg

Working across opposite side of foundation ch of body (which has one remaining free lp) and first leg, hdc in next ch, hdc2tog over next 2 ch, hdc in each of next 5 ch, 5 hdc in next ch-2 lp at end of leg, sk next sc, sc in each of next 3 sts, sc2tog over next 2 sts;

Second leg and body

Working across opposite side of foundation ch of second leg, sk first ch, sc2tog over next 2 ch, sc in each of next 3 ch, 5 hdc in next ch-2 lp at end of leg, sk next sc, hdc in each of next 4 sts, hdc2tog over next 2 sts, hdc in each of next 2 sts, sk first sc of rnd, sl st or needle-join into next st, fasten off.

Icing

With B, draw up a lp under first arm, sl st in each st around, stretching sts longer around ends of arms and legs and top of head, cut yarn and needle-join to first st of rnd.

GINGERBREAD GIRL

Rnd 1: Work same as Rnd 1 of Gingerbread Boy.

Rnd 2:

First arm

Working across opposite side of foundation ch of first arm, sc in each of next 6 free lps, 5 sc in next ch-2 lp at end of arm, sk next sc, sc in each of next 3 sts, sc2tog over next 2 sts;

Head

Working across opposite side of foundation ch of head, sk first 2 ch, sc2tog over next 2 ch, hdc in next ch, dc in next ch, 8 dc in next ch-2 lp at top of head, sk next hdc, dc in next st, hdc in next st, sc2tog over next 2 sts, sk next st;

Second arm

Working across opposite side of foundation ch of second arm, sc2tog over first 2 ch, sc in each of next 4 ch, 5 sc in next ch-2 lp at end of arm, sk next sc, sc in each of next 4 sts, sc-hdc-tog over next st and first free lp of body;

Body, skirt, and first leg

Working across opposite side of foundation ch of body (which has 1 remaining free lp) and first leg, hdc in next ch, hdc-dc-tog over next 2 ch, htr in next ch, tr in next ch, ch 2, sl st in side of tr just made, hdc in each of next 3 ch, 5 hdc in next ch-2 lp at end of leg, sk next st, sc in each of next 2 sts, draw up lp in next st, sk next st, yo and draw up lp in next st, yo, draw through 2 lps, yo draw through rem lps on hook;

Second leg and body

Working across opposite side of foundation ch of second leg, yo, draw up lp in next ch, yo draw through 2 lps on hook, sk next ch, draw up lp in next ch, yo and draw through all lps on hook (dc-sc-tog made), sc in each of next 3 ch, 5 hdc in next ch-2 lp at end of leg, sk next sc, hdc in each of next 2 sts, ch 2, tr in next st, htr in next st, dc-hdc-tog over next 2 sts, hdc2tog over next 2 sts, sk first sc of rnd, sl st or needle-join into next st, fasten off.

Icing

With B, draw up lp in first hdc of first leg, sl st in each st of leg, stretching sts longer around ends of legs—10 sts total. Fasten off B.

Draw up lp of B in first sc of second leg, sl st in each st of leg as before, sl st in next 2 ch sts, ch 1, sl st up side of skirt and body, around arms and head, down other side of skirt, ending with a st in the tr at corner of skirt, ch 1, sl st in next 2 ch, sl st across hem of skirt, holding yarn at WS of piece as you work across the top of legs, needle-join last st to the first sl-st of skirt.

FINISHING

Weave in ends. Block. If desired, add features and buttons with beads, buttons, or embroidery.

For Even More Fun...

You can do so many things with these gingerbread people around the holidays—attach to the wrappings of homemade treats for gifts, string a ribbon through them for ornaments, or sew to the corners of a tablecloth for a festive look.

snowpeople

Now you can make a snowman (or woman) even in summer. To make an ornament, either crochet another body or cut one out of felt and sew it to the back of the piece before you add the scarf. Remember to add a loop for hanging the ornament.

SKILL LEVEL
Intermediate

MATERIALS & TOOLS
4 colors of yarn: White (A), orange (B), brown or black for arms, features, and buttons (C), scarf color (D)

Crochet hook: Appropriate size hook to achieve a firm gauge with selected yarn

Tapestry needle

Embroidery floss, beads, sequins, or buttons for features if desired, with sewing needle and thread

Optional: White or clear seed beads with beading needle and thread

PATTERN NOTE
Read about free lps on page 9.

ABBREVIATIONS
Find instructions on pages 16 and 17 for: RS, htr

SNOWPERSON

With A, ch 18.

Row 1 (RS): Hdc in 3rd ch from hook, sc in each of next 2 ch, hdc in next ch, dc in each of next 2 ch, hdc in next ch, sc in next ch, hdc in next ch, dc in next ch, htr in next ch, tr in each of next 2 ch, htr in next ch, dc in next ch, ch 2 (counts as last hdc), sl st in last ch, rotate piece to work across opposite side of foundation ch—16 sts, ch-2 lp at top of head.

Rnd 2 (RS): Ch 2, dc in next ch (at base of dc), htr in next ch, tr each of next 2 ch, htr in next ch, dc in next ch, hdc in next ch, sc in next ch (waist of snowperson), hdc in next ch, dc each of next 2 ch, hdc in next ch, sc in next ch (neck of snowperson), sc in next ch, hdc in next ch, 6 hdc in next ch-2 lp at top of head, sk next hdc, sc each of next 2 sc (neck), hdc in next st, dc each of next 2 sts, hdc in next st, sc in next st (waist), hdc in next st, dc in next st, htr in

next st, tr each of next 2 sts, htr in next st, dc in next st, ch 2, sc each of next 2 ch, continue working around lower edge of snowperson.

Rnd 3 (RS):
Lower body
Sc in next st (which is a sl st from Rnd 2), sc in each of next 2 ch, (sc, hdc) in next dc, *hdc in next st, 2 hdc in next st; rep from * once, (hdc, sc) in next dc, ch 1, sk next st, sl st in next sc at waist;

Upper body
Ch 1, sk next st, (sc, hdc) in next st, (hdc, sc) in next st, ch 1, sk next st, sl st in next sc at neck;

Head
Ch 1, sk next st, *sc in next st, 2 sc in each of next 2 sts; rep from * once, sc in next st, ch 1, sk next st, sl st in next sc at neck;

Upper body
Ch 1, sk next st, (sc, hdc) in next st, (hdc, sc) in next st, ch 1, sk next st, sl st in next sc at waist;

Lower body
Ch 1, sk next st, (sc, hdc) in next st, *2 hdc in next st, hdc in next st, rep from * once, (hdc, sc) in next st, sc in next st, sl st in next st, sl st in first sc of rnd. Fasten off A.

Carrot nose
With B, ch 5, sl st in 2nd ch from hook, sl st in next ch, sc in each of next 2 ch. Fasten off B, leaving a long sewing length.

Arms
With RS facing, join C with a sl st in first hdc below the neck, ch 8, sl st in 2nd ch from hook, sl st in next ch, ch 3, sl st in 2nd ch from hook, sl st in next ch, sl st in rem ch, sl st in same st of body. Fasten off C. Repeat on other side of body.

Scarf
With D, ch 30, sc in 2nd ch from hook, *ch 1, sk next ch, sc in next ch; rep from * across. Fasten off D, leaving a long sewing length.

Buttons
With C, *ch 5, sl st in 3rd ch from hook; rep from * twice, **ch 4, sl st in 2nd ch from hook; rep from ** once, ch 2—3 large picots, 2 small picots with ch-sts between; each picot = button. Fasten off C, leaving a long sewing length.

FOR THESE SNOW PEOPLE WE USED

Dale of Norway Falk (100% superwash wool; 1¾oz/50g = 116yd/106m) DK weight yarn (3): #0017 Off-White (A), #3309 Orange (B), #0090 Black (C), #4415 Pink (D); Mill Hill beads for glisten.

GAUGE CIRCLE
(see page 7) = 1"/2.5cm worked on 4.00mm (size G-6 U.S.) hook

FINISHED MEASUREMENT
3½"/8.9cm x 3½"/8.9cm

Lion Brand Kitchen Cotton (100% cotton; 2oz/57g = 99yd/90m) medium weight yarn (4): #98 Vanilla (A), #133 Pumpkin (B), #153 Licorice (C), #106 Blueberry (D).

GAUGE CIRCLE
(see page 7) = 1¼"/3.2cm worked on 5.00mm (size H-8 U.S.) hook

FINISHED MEASUREMENT
5"/12.7cm x 5"/12.7cm

Coats & Clark Aunt Lydia's Classic Crochet Thread, No. 10, Art. 154 (100% mercerized cotton, 350yd/320m, no weight given) 10-count crochet thread (0): #428 Mint Green (A), #431 Pumpkin (B), #622 Kerry Green (C), #422 Golden Yellow (D), features embroidered with #12 Black.

GAUGE CIRCLE
(see page 7) = ⅜"/1cm worked on 2.00mm (size 4 steel U.S.) hook

FINISHED MEASUREMENT
2⅜"/6cm x 1¾"/4.4cm with antennae as shown here

Antennae

With RS facing, join A with sl st at top of head, ch 6, (2 hdc, ch 2, sl st) in 3rd ch from hook, sl st in each of next 3 ch, sl st in same st of head*, sl st in next st; rep from * to * once. Fasten off A.

FINISHING

Weave in ends except for sewing ends. Block body, scarf, and nose.

To add buttons, find central row of snowperson, then locate 2 tr in lower body. With button piece on WS of snowperson, push first large picot up between 2 tr, *skip next 2 sts, push up next picot; rep from * 3 times, using hook to help you pull them through if necessary—5 buttons with 2 sts between each pair. Use long sewing length to tack ch-sts bet picots to back of body.

With yarn or embroidery floss, embroider eyes and mouth with French knots or desired st. Sew nose in place. Weave in rem ends. For a frosty glisten, sew a few white or clear seed beads onto snowperson. Weave long end of scarf about one-fourth up length of scarf, fold scarf around neck, and use end to tack in place.

SNOWMARTIAN

Let's see, we'll need a carrot and some coal and…some antennae?? Some Martian kids created snowman Blerg when they landed on Earth during a snowstorm. They left him behind when they traveled back to Mars, but he doesn't mind; Mars is too dusty for him.

cutely
cloudy

Crocheted in white yarn, this is a sunny day cloud. If you use shaded blues or grays, you'll need the crocheted umbrella and rain boots.

INSTRUCTIONS

CLOUD

With A, ch 5, join with a sl st to form a ring.

Row 1: Ch 3 (counts as dc here and throughout), 8 dc in ring, turn—9 dc.

Row 2: Ch 3, dc in next dc, (hdc, ch 2, sl st) in next st, ch 2, hdc in next st, 2 dc in next st, (hdc, ch 2, sl st) in next st, ch 2, hdc in next st, dc in next st, htr in top of ch-3 turning ch, turn—10 sts, not counting ch-2 sps or sl sts.

Row 3: Ch 2 (counts as hdc, 2 hdc in next dc), (hdc, sc) in next hdc, ch 1, sl st in each of next 2 ch-2 spaces, ch 1, (sc, hdc) in next hdc, 2 hdc in each of next 3 sts, (hdc, sc) in next ch-2 sp, ch 1, sl st in next ch-2 sp, ch 1, (sc, hdc) in next hdc, 2 hdc in next dc, hdc in top of ch-3 turning ch, turn—20 sts, not counting ch sts or sl sts.

Row 4: Ch 7, sl st in 3rd ch from hook (counts as tr and picot), sk 1 ch, draw up a lp in next ch-st, draw up a lp in next hdc of Row 3 (3 lps on hook), yo and draw through all lps on hook (counts as hdc), 2 hdc in next st, (2 hdc, sc) in next st, sl st in next sc, sk next (ch, sl st, ch, and sc), sl st in next hdc, hdc in next st, 2 hdc in next st, (sc, sl st) in next st, (sc, hdc) in next st, (dc, htr) in next st, (htr, dc), in next st, (dc,

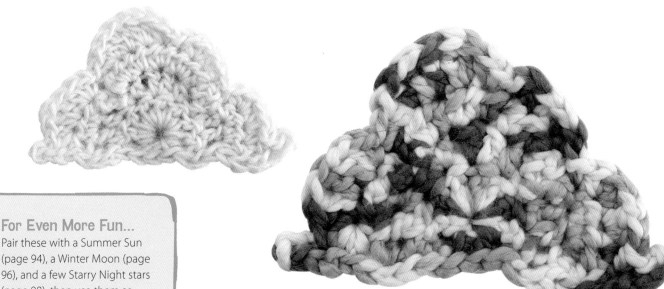

For Even More Fun...

Pair these with a Summer Sun (page 94), a Winter Moon (page 96), and a few Starry Night stars (page 98), then use them as props to tell seasonal stories to a child.

hdc) in next st, sc in next sc, sk next (ch, 2 sl sts, ch, and sc), (sc, 2 hdc) in next st, 2 dc in next hdc, 2 hdc in next hdc, ch 3, sl st in 3rd ch from hook (picot made), ch 2, sl st in top of ch-2 turning ch.

Continuing along the straight-ish lower edge of cloud, work a line of tambour sts, ending at the base of the ch-2 at beg of Row 4, cut yarn and needle-join to first ch of ch-2.

FINISHING

Weave in ends. Block.

FOR THESE CLOUDS WE USED

Lion Brand Nature's Choice Organic Cotton (100% organically grown cotton; 2.75oz/78g = 94yd/86m) medium weight yarn (**4**): #205 French Vanilla (A).

GAUGE CIRCLE
(see page 7) = 1⁷⁄₁₆"/3.6cm worked on 5.50mm (size I-9 U.S.) hook

FINISHED MEASUREMENT
5"/12.7cm wide x 3"/7.6cm tall

Lion Brand LB Collection Angora Merino (80% extra-fine merino wool, 20% angora; 1.75oz/50g = 131yd/120m) light weight yarn (**3**): #150 Smoked Pearl (A).

GAUGE CIRCLE
(see page 7) = ⁷⁄₈"/2.2cm worked on 4.00mm (size G-6 U.S.) hook

FINISHED MEASUREMENT
3⅝"/9.2cm x 2"/5.1cm

Plymouth Yarn Company Angora (100% angora; 0.36oz/10g = 49yd/44m) light weight yarn (**2**): #709 White (A).

GAUGE CIRCLE
(see page 7) = ¾"/1.9cm worked on 3.50mm (size E-4 U.S.) hook

FINISHED MEASUREMENT
3"/7.6cm x 1⅝"/4.1cm

Classic Elite Yarns Woodland (65% wool, 35% nettles; 1¾oz/50g = 131yd/100m) DK weight yarn (**3**): #3101 Ivory (A).

GAUGE CIRCLE
(see page 7) = 1"/2.5cm worked on 4.00mm (size G-6 U.S.) hook

FINISHED MEASUREMENT
3¼"/8.3cm x 1⅞"/4.8cm

spring hearts

Show your appreciation by sending a greeting card decorated with a crocheted heart! Embroider or embellish its solid center and thread a ribbon through the convenient round of filet crochet.

SKILL LEVEL
Easy

MATERIALS & TOOLS
1 color of yarn: Heart color (A)

Crochet hook: Appropriate size hook to achieve a firm gauge with selected yarn

Tapestry needle

Ribbon, embroidery floss, beads, or buttons to decorate center of heart if desired, with sewing needle and thread. I used a fray-checking adhesive on the ends of the ribbon shown here.

PATTERN NOTE
Fat picot = ch 3, hdc in 3rd ch from hook

ABBREVIATIONS
Find instructions on page 16 for: BLO

INSTRUCTIONS

RIBBON-READY HEART

With A, ch 4, join with a sl st to form a ring.

Rnd 1: Ch 3, (3 dc, hdc, sc, hdc, dc, hdc, sc, hdc, 3 dc, ch 3, sl st) in ring.

Rnd 2: Sl st in next 3 ch sts, ch 1, (hdc, dc) in next dc, 3 dc in next dc, 2 dc in next dc, dc in each of next 3 sts, 3 dc in dc at lower corner of heart, dc in each of next 3 sts, 2 dc in next dc, 3 dc in next dc, (dc, hdc) in last dc, ch 1, sl st in each of next 2 ch sts, sc in center ring.

Rnd 3: Ch 4, working in BLO around, sk next 3 sl sts, dc in next ch, ch 2, sk next st, [dc in next dc, ch 2] 3 times, [sk next st, dc in next dc, ch 2] 3 times, sk next st, (dc, ch 2, dc, ch 2, dc) in next dc (this is the middle dc of the 3 at the lower tip of the heart), [ch 2, sk next st, dc in next dc] 4 times, [ch 2, dc in next dc] twice, ch 2, sk next st, dc in next ch, ch 4, sl st in last sc of Rnd 2.

Rnd 4: Working in BLO around, sl st in each of next 4 ch, sl st in next dc, [fat picot, sl st in next dc] 16 times, sl st in next 4 ch sts, cut yarn and needle-join to first st of rnd OR fasten off.

SLIGHTLY SIMPLER HEART

If you're not planning to decorate the heart with ribbon, you may like this slightly simpler version, where the spaces created in Rnd 3 are more uniform.

Work same as Ribbon-Ready Heart through Rnd 2.

Rnd 3: Ch 4, working in BLO, sk next 3 sl sts, dc in next ch, ch 2, sk next st, [dc in next dc, ch 2] 3 times, [sk next st, dc in next dc, ch 2] 3 times, sk next st, (dc, ch 2, dc,) in next dc (this is the middle dc of the 3 at the lower corner of the heart), [ch 2, sk next st, dc in next dc] 4 times, [ch 2, dc in next dc] twice, ch 2, sk next st, dc in ch, ch 4, sl st in last sc of Rnd 2.

Rnd 4: Working in BLO, sl st in each of next 4 ch, sl st in next dc, [fat picot, sl st in next dc] 15 times, sl st in next 4 ch sts, cut yarn and needle-join to first st of rnd OR fasten off.

Garland

Crochet one heart. For each additional heart, work through Rnd 4 until only 3 fat picots remain to be done. *Ch 1, place new heart back to back with previous heart, sl st in corresponding fat picot of previous heart, ch 1, hdc in first ch to complete fat picot, sl st in next dc; rep from * once, complete Rnd 4 as usual.

These instructions produce a gently curved garland of hearts. You can join hearts however you wish to make different shapes.

FINISHING

Weave in ends. Decorate the center of the heart if desired. For Ribbon-Ready Heart, weave a narrow ribbon over and under the sts of Rnd 3 and tie in a bow at one upper corner of the heart.

FOR THESE HEARTS WE USED

Lion Brand Sock-Ease™ (75% wool, 25% nylon; 3.5oz/100g = 438yd/400m) super fine weight yarn (1): #205 Cotton Candy (A).

GAUGE CIRCLE
(see page 7) = $^{11}/_{16}$"/1.7cm worked on 3.25mm (size 0 steel U.S.) hook

FINISHED MEASUREMENT
One heart is 2¼"/5.7cm x 2"/5.1cm

Lion Brand LB Collection Cotton Bamboo (52% cotton, 48% rayon from bamboo; 3.5oz/100g = 245yd/224m) light weight yarn (3): #098 Magnolia, #138 Hibiscus, or #102 Cherry Blossom (A).

GAUGE CIRCLE
(see page 7) = 1"/2.5cm worked on 4.00mm (size G-6 U.S.) hook

FINISHED MEASUREMENT
3⅜"/8.6cm x 3"/7.6cm

seasons

nest eggs

Eggs hold the promise of new life, which is why they're so often associated with spring. Who knows what cuteness is inside, waiting to break out? Chicks, ducklings, even turtles!

SKILL LEVEL
Easy

MATERIALS & TOOLS
2 or 3 colors of yarn: Color for egg (A), nest (B)

Crochet hook: Appropriate size hook to achieve a firm gauge with selected yarn

Polyester fiberfill

Pencil with clean eraser

Tapestry needle

ABBREVIATIONS
Find instructions on pages 16 and 17 for: sc2tog over next 2 sts, FLO, BLO

FOR THESE EGGS AND NESTS WE USED

Classic Elite Yarns Majestic Tweed (40% wool, 20% angora, 20% silk, 20% nylon; 1¾oz/50g = 110yd/119m) DK weight yarn (3): #7220 Wedgewood (A), #7238 Espresso (B).

GAUGE CIRCLE
(see page 7) = 1³⁄₁₆"/3cm worked on 5.00mm (size H-8 U.S.) hook

FINISHED MEASUREMENT
Nest is 4¼"/10.8cm in diameter; egg is 1¾"/4.4cm x 1¼"/3.2cm

Dale of Norway Dale Lille Lerke (53% merino wool, 47% cotton; 1¾oz/50g = 154 yd/142m) light weight yarn (3): #6621 pale blue (A), #0020 cream (B).

GAUGE CIRCLE
(see page 7) = ¹³⁄₁₆"/2.1cm worked on 4.00mm (size G-6 U.S.) hook

FINISHED MEASUREMENT
Nest is 3¼"/8.3cm in diameter; egg is 1³⁄₈"/3.5cm x ⅞"/2.2cm

EGG

With A, ch 4, join with sl st to first ch to form a ring.

Rnd 1: Ch 1, 5 sc in ring, join with sl st in first sc—5 sc.

Rnd 2: Ch 1, 2 sc in each sc around, join with sl st in first sc—10 sc.

Rnd 3: Ch 1, starting in first st, *sc in each of next 4 sts, 2 sc in next st; rep from * once, join with sl st in first sc—12 sc.

Rnds 4 and 5: Ch 1, sc in each sc around, join with sl st in first sc—12 sc.

Rnd 6: Ch 1, starting in first st, *sc in each of next 4 sts, sc2tog over next 2 sts; rep from * once, join with sl st in first sc—10 sc.

Rnd 7: Ch 1, starting in first st, *sc in each of next 2 sts, sc2tog over next 2 sts, sc in next st; rep from * once, join with sl st in first sc—8 sc.

Rnd 8: Ch 1, starting in first st, *sc2tog over next 2 sts, sc in each of next 2 sts; rep from * once, join with sl st in first sc—6 sc.

FINISHING

Lightly stuff egg with fiberfill: Insert hook from side or bottom of egg and out the top opening, hook the fiberfill into the egg, then use the eraser end of the pencil to stuff remaining fiberfill into the egg. Thread yarn onto a tapestry needle, stitch across the opening and under the tops of sts of the last rnd in this order: 3rd, 6th, 2nd, 5th, 1st, and 4th from the beg of rnd. Tack yarn. Weave in ends.

NEST

With B, ch 5, join with sl st in first ch to form a ring.

Rnd 1: Ch 2 (counts as hdc here and throughout), 7 hdc in ring, join with sl st in top of beg ch-2—8 hdc.

Rnd 2: Ch 2 hdc in first st, 2 hdc in each of next 7 sts, join with sl st in top of beg ch-2—16 hdc.

Rnd 3: Ch 2, hdc in first st, 2 hdc in each of next 15 sts, join with sl st in top of beg ch-2—32 hdc.

Rnd 4: Ch 2, hdc in each hdc around, join with sl st in top of beg ch-2—32 hdc.

Rnd 5: Working in BLO of sts in Rnd 4, *sk 1 st, 5 hdc in next st, sk 1 st, sl st in next st; rep from * 7 times—8 shells.

Rnd 6: Ch 2, working in FLO of sts in Rnd 4, hdc in each hdc around, join with sl st in top of beg ch-2—32 hdc.

Rnd 7: Sl st in each of next 2 sts, working in BLO of sts in Rnd 6, *sk 1 st, 5 hdc in next st, sk 1 st, sl st in next st; rep from * 6 times, sk 1 st, 5 hdc in next st, sk 1 st, sl st in FL of next st—8 shells.

Rnd 8: Ch 1, working in FLO of sts in Rnd 6, sc in each st around, cut yarn and needle-join to first st of rnd—32 sc.

FINISHING

Weave in ends. Place 3 small eggs in nest.

valentine roses

My daughter Ella's drawings of rosebud bouquets gave me the idea for the quick and simple Spiral Rosebud, while bullion embroidery inspired the more challenging Bullion Rose.

SKILL LEVEL
Intermediate

MATERIALS & TOOLS
2 colors of yarn: Rose color (A), leaf color (B)

Crochet hook: Appropriate size hook to achieve a firm gauge with selected yarn

Tapestry needle

Embroidery floss, beads, or buttons to decorate center of flower, with sewing needle and thread

PATTERN NOTE
Read about bullion st on page 11.

ABBREVIATIONS
Find instructions on page 17 for: PM, RM

INSTRUCTIONS

SPIRAL ROSEBUD
With A, ch 5.

Row 1 (RS): Sc in 2nd ch from hook, sc in each of next 3 ch, do not turn—4 sc.

Rnd 2 (RS): Ch 6, 3 sc in 2nd ch from hook, 3 hdc in next ch, 3 dc in next st, PM in first dc of this group, 3 dc in each of next 2 sts (spiral finished), working across opposite side of foundation ch of Row 1, dc in each of next 2 ch, hdc in next ch, 2 sc in next ch, ch 1, rotate piece to work across sts in Row 1, 2 sc in first sc, hdc in next sc, dc in each of next 2 sc, sl st in back of st with marker, placing st in lp immediately under and behind the top 2 lps of st, RM. Fasten off.

Greenery
With B, ch 4, sl st in 3rd ch from hook, sc in next ch, ch 4, sl st in 3rd ch from hook, (sc, hdc) in next ch, ch 20 or desired length of stem, sc in 2nd ch from hook, sl st in each ch across to last ch, sk last ch, sl st to first ch of greenery. Fasten off, leaving a long sewing length.

FINISHING
Weave in ends except for sewing length. Block gently. Sew greenery to lower end of rosebud.

BULLION ROSE
Rnd 1 (Center Petal 1): With A, ch 5, wrap yarn 12 times around hook, draw up lp in 5th ch from hook and through all wraps on hook, ch 1 to lock bullion st, pull thread tight in order to curve bullion

st so its top and bottom meet—resulting bullion picot will lie on top of ch-5.

Rnd 2:

Petal 2: Ch 5, wrap yarn 12 times around hook, draw up lp in 5th ch from hook and through all wraps on hook, sl st in very first ch of Center Petal 1 which completes locking-st—2 bullion sts joined at base;

Petal 3: Ch 5, wrap yarn 12 times around hook, draw up lp in 5th ch from hook and through all wraps on hook, sl st in ch-5 lp behind Center Petal 1 which completes locking-st;

Petal 4: Ch 5, wrap yarn 12 times around hook, draw up lp in 5th ch from hook and through all wraps on hook, sl st in first ch of Petal 2.

Rnd 3: (This rnd continues in the established direction.)

Petal 5: Ch 6, wrap yarn 15 times around hook, draw up lp in 6th ch from hook and through all wraps on hook, sl st under ch-5 lp behind Petal 3 in rnd that completes locking-st;

Petal 6: Ch 6, wrap yarn 15 times around hook, draw up lp in 6th ch from hook and through all wraps on hook, sl st under ch-5 lp behind next petal in rnd that completes locking-st;

Petal 7: Ch 6, wrap yarn 15 times around hook, draw up lp in 6th ch from hook and through all wraps on hook, sl st under ch-6 lp of SAME petal as last time that completes locking-st;

Petal 8: Rep Petal 6;

Petal 9: Ch 6, wrap yarn 15 times around hook, draw up lp in 6th ch from hook and through all wraps on hook, sl st into st at base of first petal of this rnd (Petal 5). Fasten off.

Leaf

With B, ch 7.

Rnd 1: Hdc in 3rd ch from hook, dc in next ch, hdc in next ch, sc in next ch, (sl st, ch 1, sl st) in next ch, rotate piece to work across opposite side of foundation ch, sc in next ch, hdc in next ch, dc in next ch, (hdc, ch 1, sl st) in next ch. Fasten off, leaving a long sewing length.

FINISHING

Weave in ends, except for sewing length. Sew leaf to back of Bullion Rose, so its tip peeks out behind the last rnd of petals.

FOR THESE ROSES WE USED

Lion Brand LB Collection Angora Merino (80% extra-fine merino wool, 20% angora; 1.75oz/50g = 131yd/120m) light weight yarn : #103 Blossom (A), #174 Avocado (B).

GAUGE CIRCLE
(see page 7) = ⅞"/2.2cm worked on 4.00mm (size G-6 U.S.) hook

FINISHED MEASUREMENT
1⅛"/2.9cm x 5¼"/13.3cm with stem

Lion Brand LB Collection Cotton Bamboo (52% cotton, 48% rayon from bamboo; 3.5oz/100g = 245yd/224m) light weight yarn : #102 Cherry Blossom or #139 Hibiscus (A), #174 Snapdragon (B).

GAUGE CIRCLE
(see page 7) = 1"/2.5cm worked on 4.00mm (size G-6 U.S.) hook

FINISHED MEASUREMENT
1⅛"/2.9cm x 5⅛"/13cm with stem

Plymouth Yarn Company Plymouth Select Worsted Merino Superwash (100% superwash fine merino wool; 3.5oz/100g = 218yd/198m) medium weight yarn : #57 Lipstick or #38 Gulden (A), #36 Lichen (B).

GAUGE CIRCLE
(see page 7) = 1"/2.5cm worked on 5.00mm (size H-8 U.S.) hook

FINISHED MEASUREMENT
2⅛"/5.4cm across

summer sun

After the dark and chill of night, we welcome the light and warmth of the sun. It's easy to understand why people through the ages have imagined the sun smiling down upon us.

SKILL LEVEL
Easy

MATERIALS & TOOLS
1 or more colors of yarn: Sun color (A), sun's face and trim color (B)

Crochet hook: Appropriate size hook to achieve a firm gauge with selected yarn

Tapestry needle

PATTERN NOTES
Read about needle-joining (page 10), tambour st (page 11), and free lps (page 9).

ABBREVIATIONS
Find instructions on page 16 for: BLO

FOR THESE SUNS WE USED

Berroco Captiva (60% cotton, 23% polyester, 17% acrylic; 1.75oz/50g = 98yd/90m) medium weight yarn (4): #5520 Honey (A).

> **GAUGE CIRCLE**
> (see page 7) = almost 1"/2.5cm worked on 4.00mm (size G-6 U.S.) hook
>
> **FINISHED MEASUREMENT**
> (clubby sunrays) 3¾"/9.5cm in diameter

Cascade 220 Sport (100% Peruvian Highland wool; 1.75oz/50g = 164yd/15m) light weight yarn (3): #7827 Goldenrod (A), #7825 Orange Sherbet (B).

> **GAUGE CIRCLE**
> (see page 7) = ⅞"/2.2cm worked on 3.50mm (size E-4 U.S.) hook
>
> **FINISHED MEASUREMENT**
> (spiky sunrays) 3⅜"/8.6cm in diameter

Classic Elite Yarns Liberty Wool (100% washable wool; 1¾oz/50g = 122yd/111m) DK/sport weight yarn (3): #7880 Golden Poppy (A).

Cloud pattern is on page 00, worked in same yarn, color Bleach #7801.

> **GAUGE CIRCLE**
> (see page 7) = ⅞"/2.2cm worked on 4.00mm (size G-6 U.S.) hook
>
> **FINISHED MEASUREMENT**
> 3⅞"/9.8cm for sun, 3½"/8.9cm x 1⅞"/4.8cm for cloud

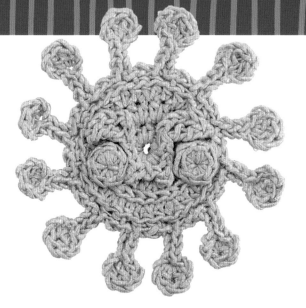

INSTRUCTIONS

SUN

With A, ch 5, join with a sl st to form a ring.

Rnd 1: Ch 2 (counts as hdc here and throughout), 11 hdc in ring, join with sl st in top of beg ch-2—12 hdc.

Rnd 2: Ch 2, hdc in first st, 2 hdc in next 11 sts, join with sl st in top of beg ch-2—24 hdc.

Rnd 3: Ch 2, hdc in first st, hdc in next st, *2 hdc in next st, hdc in next st; rep from * 10 times, join with sl st in BL of 2nd ch of ch-2 at beg of rnd—36 hdc.

SUNRAY VARIATIONS

Clubby Sunrays

Rnd 4: Working in BLO, *ch 6, (2 dc, ch 2, sl st) in 3rd ch from hook, sl st in each of next 3 ch, sl st in same st of Rnd 3, ch 2, sk next 2 sts of Rnd 3, sl st in next st of Rnd 3; rep from * 11 times, fasten off yarn OR unravel last sl st, cut yarn and needle-join to first st of rnd—12 sunrays.

Spiky Sunrays

Rnd 4: Working in BLO, *ch 6, sl st in 2nd ch from hook, working down ch, sc in next ch, hdc in next ch, dc in next ch, htr in next ch, sk next 3 sts of Rnd 3, sl st in

next st of Rnd 3; rep from * 8 times, fasten off yarn OR unravel last sl st, cut yarn and needle-join to first st of rnd—9 sunrays.

OPTIONAL RND 5 FOR SPIKY SUNRAYS

Join A or B with sl st in sl st bet any two sunrays of Rnd 3 (stitch over the sl st that is already there), working up free lps of ch of next sunray, sk first ch, sl st in in next ch (with dc in it), sl st in next ch (with hdc in it), sl st in next ch (with sc in it), sl st in next ch (with sl-st in it), sl st in ch-1 at tip of sunray, ch 1, working down other side of sunray, sk next sl st, sl st in next sc, sl st in each of next 3 sts, sl st in next sl st between rays; rep from * 8 times, fasten off yarn OR unravel last sl st, cut yarn and needle-join to first st of rnd—9 outlined sunrays.

Sun Cheeks (make 2)

With A or B, ch 4, join with sl st to form ring.

Rnd 1: Ch 1, 6 sc in ring, leaving long end for sewing, cut yarn and needle-join to first sc of rnd—6 sc.

Sun Eyes and Nose

With A or B, ch 6, tr in 6th ch from hook (first eye complete); *ch 5, remove hook from lp, insert hook into 3rd ch from lp,

reinsert hook into free lp and pull through ch; rep from * once to complete nose; ch 8, tr in 6th ch from hook (second eye complete). Fasten off, leaving a long sewing length.

FINISHING

Weave in ends of sun and block.

Smile: With RS of sun face, insert hook in top of any st of Rnd 2 (this st will have st or sts from Rnd 3 in it already), at WS of face, yo with A or B and pull up a lp to RS, work tambour sts into next 8 sts of Rnd 2, cut yarn, pull end through last tambour st, then use hook or tapestry needle to pull end to WS of face. Sew cheeks over ends of smile. Try different placements for eyes and nose before sewing in place. With sewing length, sew eyes and nose in place through back lps of ch-sts. Weave in ends.

winter moon

Even the coldest winter's night feels a bit more cheery when you look up and see the Man in the Moon is there to keep you company.

For Even More Fun...
Use these moons to teach a young child a simple science lesson about lunar phases, or attach them, along with a smattering of Starry Nights stars (page 98), to a bedroom ceiling for a cosmic show before lights out.

SKILL LEVEL
Easy

MATERIALS & TOOLS
1 color of yarn: Moon (A)

Crochet hook: Appropriate size hook to achieve a firm gauge with selected yarn

Tapestry needle

ABBREVIATIONS
Find instructions on pages 16 and 17 for: dc2tog, hdc2tog, sc2tog

FOR THESE MOONS WE USED

Lion Brand LB Collection Cotton Bamboo (52% cotton, 48% rayon from bamboo; 3.5oz/100g = 245yd/224m) light weight yarn (3): #098 Magnolia (A).

GAUGE CIRCLE
(see page 7) = 1"/2.5cm worked on 4.00mm (size G-6 U.S.) hook

FINISHED MEASUREMENT
3"/7.6cm x 1½"/3.8cm for crescent moon

Lion Brand Nature's Choice Organic Cotton (100% organically grown cotton; 2.75oz/78g = 94yd/86m) medium weight yarn (4): #108 Blueberry (A).

GAUGE CIRCLE
(see page 7) = 1⁷⁄₁₆"/3.6cm worked on 5.50mm (size I-9 U.S.) hook

FINISHED MEASUREMENT
3¼"/8.3cm in diameter for full moon

INSTRUCTIONS

CRESCENT MOON

With A, ch 24.

Row 1: Sl st in 2nd ch from hook, sc in each of next 2 sts, sc2tog over next 2 ch, sc in next st, hdc2tog over next 2 ch, hdc in next st, dc2tog over next 2 ch, dc in next st, dc2tog over next 2 ch, hdc in next ch, hdc2tog over next 2 ch, sc in next st, sc2tog over next 2 ch, sc in each of next 2 ch, sl st in next ch, do not turn—18 sts, 2 ch.

Rnd 2: Ch 2, rotate piece to work across opposite side of foundation ch, sl st in first ch at base of sl st, sl st in each of next 22 ch,

taking care to enlarge sts when necessary to keep piece flat, sl st in next ch, ch 2, rotate piece to work along sts of Rrow 1, sl st in each of next 16 sts, ch 2, cut yarn and needle-join to first sl st of rnd.

FULL MOON

Work same as for "Summer Sun" (page 94), through Rnd 3, fasten off or needle-join. Add facial features if desired.

For a larger moon, work Rnds 1-3 as above, but do not cut yarn, continue to Rnd 4.

Rnd 4: Ch 2 (counts hdc), *(2 hdc) in next st, hdc in each of next 2 sts; rep from * 10 times, 2 hdc in next st, hdc in next st, join with sl st in top of ch-2 at beg of rnd and fasten off OR cut yarn and needle-join to first st in rnd—48 hdc.

FINISHING

Weave in ends. Block. Add a cat, a cloud, or tree branches for a lovely autumn scene.

starry night

I was a proud and happy first-grader when I finally mastered drawing a five-pointed star without lifting my pencil. Here's a crocheted version of my elementary school star, along with two more stars to spangle your summer nights.

SKILL LEVEL
Intermediate

MATERIALS & TOOLS
1 color of yarn: Star color (A)

Crochet hook: Appropriate size hook to achieve a firm gauge with selected yarn

For Elementary School Star: Tracing or photocopy of 5-point template (page 144), with points extended to fit your star, pins

Tapestry needle

ABBREVIATIONS
Find instructions on pages 16 and 17 for: RS, htr, PM, dc2tog, dc-hdc-tog

FOR THESE STARS WE USED
Dale of Norway Falk (100% superwash wool; 1¾oz/50g = 116yd/106m) DK weight yarn (3): #0017 Off-White, #5624 Blue Bell, or #5545 Deep Blue (A).

GAUGE CIRCLE
(see page 7) = 1"/2.5cm worked on 4.00mm (size G-6 U.S.) hook

FINISHED MEASUREMENT
3½"/8.9cm in diameter for Elementary School Star

Lion Brand Kitchen Cotton (100% cotton; 2oz/57g = 99yd/90m) medium weight yarn (4): #113 Hot Pepper, #170 Kiwi, #157 Citrus, or #133 Pumpkin (A).

GAUGE CIRCLE
(see page 7) = 1¼"/3.2cm worked on 5.00mm (size H-8 U.S.) hook

FINISHED MEASUREMENT
2¼"/5.7cm in diameter for Small Star

Lion Brand Sock-Ease™ (75% wool, 25% nylon; 3.5oz/100g = 438yd/400m) super fine weight yarn (1): #204 Lemon Drop (A).

GAUGE CIRCLE
(see page 7) = ¹¹⁄₁₆"/1.7cm worked on 3.25mm (size 0 steel U.S.) hook

FINISHED MEASUREMENT
3"/7.6cm in diameter for Pinwheel Star— this star has an outline rnd

Plymouth Yarn Company Plymouth Select Worsted Merino Superwash (100% superwash fine merino wool; 3.5oz/100g = 218yd/198m) medium weight yarn (4): #38 Gulden (A).

GAUGE CIRCLE
(see page 7) = 1"/2.5cm worked on 5.00mm (size H-8 U.S.) hook

FINISHED MEASUREMENT
4"/10.2cm in diameter for Pinwheel Star—this star has no outline rnd

INSTRUCTIONS

ELEMENTARY SCHOOL STAR

Using A, ch 67.

Row 1 (RS): Dc in 4th ch from hook (ch lp counts as one dc), dc in each of next 3 ch, *(dc, htr, 2 ch, htr, dc) in next ch, dc in each of next 12 ch; rep from * 3 times, (dc, htr, 2 ch, htr, dc) in next ch, dc in each of next 7 ch. Fasten off, leaving long sewing length.

Using the tracing or photocopy of the Elementary School Star template on page 144, pin first crocheted point, RS up, at point A; untwisting piece as necessary, pin next crocheted point at point B, forming first leg of star; pin next crocheted point at point C, forming second leg of star; on your way to line D, slip rem length of Row 1 under first leg of star, then pin next crocheted point at point D; on your way to point E, take rem length of Row 1 over first leg of star and under second leg of star, pin last crocheted point at point E; take rem length of Row 1 over second leg of star, sew beg of Row 1 to end of Row 1 underneath first leg of star.

SMALL STAR

Using A, ch 5, join with sl st to form ring.

Rnd 1: Ch 1, 10 sc in ring, join with sl st to first sc of rnd—10 sc.

Rnd 2: *Ch 4, sl st in 2nd ch from hook, sc in next ch, hdc in next ch, sk next st of Rnd 1, sl st in next st of Rnd 1; rep from * 4 times, fasten off yarn OR unravel last sl st, cut yarn and needle-join to first st of rnd.

PINWHEEL STAR

Pattern Note: The WS of a chain is the side with bumps on it. Each point of this star is worked from the center out and back again, twice. When you are working back toward the center, you are looking at RS of star.

With A, ch 5, join with sl st to form ring.

Point 1

Ch 12, PM in 9th ch from hook, sl st in 2nd ch from hook, working down ch toward center ring, sc in each of next 2 ch, hdc in each of next 2 ch, dc2tog over next 2 ch, dc-hdc-tog over next 2 ch, hdc in next ch, sc in next ch, sl st in ring, ch 1, turn, sl st in sc and in each of next 7 sts, sl st in ch at tip of point, turn, ch 11, sl st in ring.

Point 2

Turn, ch 1, looking at WS of ch, sl st in each of first 4 ch, ch 8, sl st in 2nd ch from hook, working down ch, sc in each of next 2 ch, hdc in each of next 2 ch, dc2tog over next 2 ch, dc-hdc-tog over next 2 sl sts, hdc in next sl st, sc in next sl st, sl st in ring, ch 1, turn, sl st in sc and in each of next 7 sts, sl st in ch at tip of point, turn, ch 11, sl st in ring.

Point 3

Rep Point 2.

Point 4

Rep Point 2.

Point 5

Turn, ch 1, sl st in each of first 4 ch, ch 8, sl st in 2nd ch from hook, working down ch, sc in each of next 2 ch, hdc in each of next 2 ch, dc2tog over next 2 ch, dc-hdc-tog over next 2 ch, hdc in next ch, sc in next ch, sl st in ring, ch 1, turn, sl st in sc and in each of next 7 sts, sl st in ch at tip of point, turn, ch 7, sl st in st of Point 1 which has a marker in it, turn to WS, continuing toward center ring, sl st in each of next 3 ch (these are free lps from ch-12 at beg of Point 1), sl st in ring. Fasten off.

Optional Outline Round

Draw up lp in st where two points meet, working out toward next point, *sl st in free lps of each of next 8 ch, sc-picot at tip of point, working toward center of star, sl st in each of next 7 ch; rep from * around, cut yarn and needle-join to first sl st of rnd.

FINISHING

Weave in ends. Dampen stars, pin to ironing surface, and steam block. When pieces are dry, remove pins.

archy cat

A bowed-up cat is a traditional symbol of Halloween, especially in front of a full moon.

SKILL LEVEL
Intermediate

MATERIALS & TOOLS
1 or 2 colors of yarn: Cat color (A), optional moon color (B)

Crochet hook: Appropriate size hook to achieve a firm gauge with selected yarn

Tapestry needle

ABBREVIATIONS
Find instructions on pages 16 and 17 for: htr, PM, RM, RS, slst-picot

CAT WITH TAIL DOWN

With A, ch 9.

Row 1: *Draw up lp in 2nd ch from hook, draw up lp in each of next 2 ch and pull lp through all 4 lps on hook (sc3tog made), sl st in each of next 2 ch, sc2tog over next 2 ch, hdc in next ch* (hind leg made), ch 14, rep from * to * once (front leg made), (hdc, dc) in next ch, 2 dc in each of next 4 ch, sl st in first ch of original ch-9, turn.

Row 2: Ch 11, sl st in 2nd ch from hook, sl st in each of next 5 ch, 2 sl st in each of next 2 ch, sl st in next 2 ch, working along curve of back, sk first dc, sl st in next dc, sc in next dc, (sc, hdc) in next dc, hdc in next dc, 2 hdc in next dc, hdc in next dc, 2 sc in next st, sl st in next st. Fasten off A.

Head

With A, ch 4, join with sl st to first ch to form ring, ch 1, 3 sc in ring, slst-picot, sl st in ring, slst-picot, 3 sc in ring, join with sl st in first sc. Fasten off, leaving long sewing length.

CAT WITH TAIL UP

With A, ch 9.

Row 1: *Draw up lp in 2nd ch from hook, draw up lp in each of next 2 ch and pull lp through all 4 lps on hook (sc3tog made), sl st in each of next 2 ch, sc2tog over next 2 ch, hdc in next ch* (hind leg made), ch 14, rep from * to * once (front leg made), (hdc, dc) in next ch, 2 dc in each of next 4 ch, sl st in first ch of original ch-9, turn.

Row 2: Ch 1, sc in first dc, ch 11, sl st in 2nd ch from hook, sl st in next ch, sk next ch, sl st in each of next 3 ch, sk next ch, sl st in each of next 2 ch, draw up lp in next ch, draw up lp in next dc of cat's back and pull lp through all lps on hook, (sc, hdc) in next dc, hdc in next dc, 2 hdc in next dc, hdc in next dc, 2 sc in next st, sl st in next st. Fasten off A.

Make head same as for other cat.

FINISHING

Turn cat body to face in desired direction, sew head to body near last sl st of body, using photo as a guide for placement. Weave in remaining ends; block. If desired, crochet a full moon (see page 96) and sew cat to front of moon.

FOR THIS CAT WE USED

Lion Brand Kitchen Cotton (100% cotton; 2oz/57g = 99yd/90m) medium weight yarn (**4**): #153 Licorice and #133 Pumpkin (A), #157 Citrus (B).

GAUGE CIRCLE
(see page 7) = 1¼"/3.2cm worked on 5.00mm (size H-8 U.S.) hook

FINISHED MEASUREMENT
3⅜"/8.6cm wide x 2¾"/7cm tall for cat with tail down, 3"/7.6cm wide x 3⅜"/8.6cm tall for cat with tail up

seasons

wreath with berries and bow

Change the colors to make a wreath for any season. You can substitute beads, tiny crocheted flowers (see Gardening Hat on page 64), or embroidery for the crocheted berries.

SKILL LEVEL
Intermediate

MATERIALS & TOOLS
2 colors of yarn: Berry color (A), wreath color (B)

Crochet hook: Appropriate size hook to achieve a firm gauge with selected yarn

Tapestry needle

ABBREVIATIONS
Find instructions on page 16 for: BL, FL

INSTRUCTIONS

WREATH
With A, ch 4.

Row 1: Sc in 2nd ch from hook, hdc in next ch, dc in last ch, turn—3 sts.

Row 2: Ch 5, sl st in BL of first dc, ch 4, sl st in BL of next hdc, ch 4, sl st in BL of next sc, ch 1, before you turn, identify the FLs of the three sts you worked into in this row, as you turn keep in mind where those FLs are, okay, turn!—3 ch-lps.

Row 3: Fold ch-lps out of the way toward you. Stitching into the unworked lps you identified in the prev row, sc in first st, hdc in next st, dc in next st, turn—3 sts.

Row 4: Ch 5, sl st in BL of first dc, ch 4, sl st in BL of next hdc, ch 4, sl st in BL of next sc, ch 1, before you turn, identify the FLs

of the three sts you worked into in this row because you will be working in them in the next row, turn—3 ch-lps.

Rows 5–36: Rep Rows 3 and 4 until you have 18 rows of ch-lps. Fasten off A, leaving a long sewing length.

Berries

With B, *ch 3, slst-picot; rep from * until you have 9 (or desired number of) picots, ch 3. Fasten off B, leaving a long sewing length.

Bow

Row 1: With B, ch 5, hdc in 3rd ch from hook, sc in next ch, sl st in next ch, turn—3 sts.

Row 2: Ch 1, sk sl-st of prev row, sc in next st, turn—1 sc.

Row 3: Ch 3, hdc in 3rd ch from hook, sc in next sc, sl st in ch-1 at beg of prev row—3 sts.

Rows 4–6: Rep Rows 1–3. Join with sl st to first st of Row 1 (bow complete).

Row 7: Ch 8, hdc in 3rd ch from hook, sc in next ch, sl st in each of next 4 ch (first ribbon streamer done), ch 8, hdc in 3rd ch from hook, sc in next ch, sk next ch, sl st in rem 3 ch (2nd ribbon streamer done).

Row 8: Turn so that bow is up, ribbon streamers down. Inserting hook over middle of bow (not into any st, just over the top), yo, pull through lp on hook, *draw up a lp from between ribbon streamers, yo, pull through all lps on hook to complete sc; rep from * once. Fasten off B, leaving a long sewing length.

FINISHING

Fold last row of ch-lps of the wreath out of the way to the front, match the FLs of the last Row 3 to the corresponding free lps of the foundation ch, using sewing length of A, sew sts together. Weave in ends.

Hold strand of picots on WS of wreath. Every other row or however often you wish, use hook to pull a picot through to the front of the wreath to resemble berries. When you are satisfied with the arrangement of berries, use sewing length of B to sew ch at back of wreath.

Place bow on RS of either top or bottom of wreath, and use sewing length of B to sew in place.

crayons

The smell of fresh crayons is one of the joys of starting a new school year. Let these plump crocheted ones remind you of the many possibilities and memories in a box of crayons.

SKILL LEVEL
Easy

MATERIALS & TOOLS
3 colors of yarn: Crayon color (A), white, light gray, or very pale version of crayon color (B), black or dark version of crayon color (C)

Crochet hook: Appropriate size hook to achieve a firm gauge with selected yarn

Polyester fiberfill

Tapestry needle

PATTERN NOTE
Stuff yarn ends into crayon as you go. The crayon is stuffed lightly to preserve the cylindrical shape with a flat bottom and pointy top.

ABBREVIATIONS
Find instructions on page 16 for:
BL, BLO

FOR THESE CRAYONS WE USED
Dale of Norway Falk (100% superwash wool; 1¾oz/50g = 116yd/106m) DK weight yarn (3): #4536 dark pink or #5646 royal blue (A), #4415 pale pink or #5624 pale blue (B), #0090 black (C).

GAUGE CIRCLE
(see page 7) = 1"/2.5cm worked on 4.00mm (size G-6 U.S.) hook

FINISHED MEASUREMENT
1"/2.5cm in diameter x 3⅞"/9.8cm long

For Even More Fun...
Attach seven or eight of these crayons to fishing wire, then suspend from a hoop to create a cute mobile for a baby's room!

INSTRUCTIONS

CRAYON

Using A, ch 4, join with a sl st to form a ring.

Rnd 1: Ch 2 (counts as hdc here and throughout), 11 hdc in ring, join with sl st in top of beg ch-2—12 hdc.

Rnd 2: Ch 2, working in BLO, hdc in each st around, join with sl st in top of beg ch-2—12 hdc. Fasten off A.

Rnd 3: With RS facing, join B with sl st in any st in Rnd 2, sl st in each st around join with sl st in first sl st of rnd—12 sl sts.

Rnd 4: Ch 2, working in BLO, hdc in each st around, join with sl st to top of beg ch-2, open the last lp wide, pass skein of yarn through lp and tighten lp, do not cut yarn—12 hdc.

Rnd 5: With RS facing, join C with sc in any st of Rnd 2, sc in each st around, join with sl st in first sc—12 sc. Fasten off C.

Rnd 6: Draw up B from rnd below and sl st in nearest st of Rnd 5, ch 2, hdc in each st around, join with sl st in top of beg ch-2—12 hdc.

Rnds 7–9: Ch 2, hdc in each st around, join with sl st in top of beg ch-2—12 hdc. Stuff crayon lightly.

Rnd 10: Ch 2, hdc in each st around, join with sl st in top of beg ch-2, open the last lp wide, pass skein of yarn through lp and tighten lp, do not cut yarn—12 hdc.

Rnd 11: With RS facing, join C with sc in any st in Rnd 10, sc in next 11 sts, join with sl st in first sc—12 sc. Fasten off C.

Rnd 12: Draw up B from rnd below and sl st in nearest st of Rnd 11, ch 2, hdc in each st around, join with sl st in top of beg ch-2—12 hdc. Fasten off B.

Rnd 13: With RS facing, working in BLO, join A with hdc in st in Rnd 12, hdc in each st around, join with sl st in first hdc—12 hdc. Stuff crayon lightly to top of rnd.

Rnd 14: Ch 1, working in BLO, [sc2tog over next 2 sts] 6 times, join with sl st in first st—6 sts. Add a little fiberfill.

Rnd 15: Ch 2, [dc2tog over next 2 sts] twice, stuff point with a tiny amount of fiberfill, dc2tog, sk ch-2 at beg of rnd, sl st in next st. Fasten off A, leaving a long sewing length.

FINISHING

If necessary, make one tacking st in top of crayon to close the point completely. Weave in ends.

baby carriage

Imagine nursery curtains with a border of baby carriages parading along in all colors. If you need a last-minute baby shower gift, personalize a purchased baby blanket with a crocheted baby carriage appliqué.

SKILL LEVEL
Easy

MATERIALS & TOOLS
3 colors of yarn: Carriage color (A), spoke color (B), tire color (C)

Crochet hook: Appropriate size hook to achieve a firm gauge with selected yarn

Tapestry needle

PATTERN NOTE
Read about tambour st on page 11.

ABBREVIATIONS
Find instructions on page 16 for: htr

FOR THESE BABY CARRIAGES WE USED

Lion Brand LB Collection Angora Merino (80% extra-fine merino wool, 20% angora; 1.75oz/50g = 131yd/120m) light weight yarn (**3**): #103 Blossom and #108 Blue Bonnet (A), #150 Smoked Pearl (B) and (C).

GAUGE CIRCLE
(see page 7) = ⅞"/2.2cm worked on 4.00mm (size G-6 U.S.) hook

FINISHED MEASUREMENT
3"/7.6cm wide x 3¼"/8.3cm tall, excluding handle. Height varies depending on placement of wheels.

Cascade Ultra Pima Fine (100% pima cotton; 1.75oz/50g = 136.7yd/125m) sport weight yarn (**2**): #3762 Spring Green (A), #3743 Yellow Rose (B), #3728 White (C).

GAUGE CIRCLE
(see page 7) = ¾"/1.9cm worked on 3.50mm (size E-4 U.S.) hook

Baby Martian crocheted with No. 10 crochet cotton: Green.

FINISHED MEASUREMENT
2¾"/7cm x 3"/7.6cm, excluding handle. Height varies depending on placement of wheels.

INSTRUCTIONS

BABY CARRIAGE

With A, ch 5, join with sl st to form ring.

Row 1: Ch 3 (counts as dc here and throughout), (6 dc, 3 hdc, dc, htr, tr) in ring, turn—12 sts.

Row 2: Ch 4 (counts as tr), tr in first st, 2 tr in next st, 2 htr in next st, (dc, hdc) in next st, hdc in each of next 2 sts, 2 hdc in next st, 2 dc in each of next 5 sts, dc in top of ch-4 turning ch, turn—23 sts (counting turning ch as 1 tr).

Row 3: Ch 3, dc in first st, [dc in next st, 2 dc in next st] 5 times, 2 hdc in next st, hdc in each of next 5 sts, 2 hdc in next st, dc in next st, (dc, htr) in next st, htr in next st, (htr, tr) in next st, tr in top of ch-4 turning ch.

Row 4: To make handle, ch 10, sl st in 2nd ch from hook, sl st in each of next 2 sts, [ch 1, sl st in next st] 3 times, sl st in each of next 2 ch, sk next ch-st, sl st in side of last tr of Row 3; work sl sts across the side of the tr and along the edge to the corner, sl st into original ring, rotate piece, work sl sts up the next edge, cut yarn and needle-join to first dc of Row 3.

Wheels (Make 2)

With B, ch 4, join with sl st to form ring.

Rnd 1: Ch 5 (counts as dc, ch 2), *dc in ring, ch 2; rep from * 6 times, join with sl st to 3rd ch of beg ch-5. Fasten off B.

Rnd 2: With RS facing, join C with sc in any ch-2 sp of Rnd 1, 2 sc in same sp, 3 sc in each ch-2 sp around, cut yarn and needle-join to first st of rnd.

FINISHING

Sew wheels to lower edge of carriage as shown in photo. Weave in ends. Block.

drums

These sweet little drums would make lovely holiday ornaments— just attach a pretty ribbon and hang them from your tree.

DRUM

With A, ch 9.

Row 1: Draw up a lp in 2nd ch from hook, draw up a lp in next ch, yo, draw through all 3 lps on hook (sc2tog made), sc in each of next 5 ch, 2 sc in next ch, turn—8 sc.

Row 2: Ch 1, 2 sc in first sc, sc in each of next 5 sts, sc2tog over last 2 sts, turn—8 sc.

Row 3: Ch 1, sc2tog over first 2 sts, sc in each of next 5 sts, 2 sc in last st, turn—8 sc.

Rows 4–8: Ch 1, sc in each st across, ch 1, turn—8 sc.

Row 9: Ch 1, 2 sc in first sc, sc in each of next 5 sts, sc2tog over last 2 sts, turn—8 sc.

Row 10: Ch 1, sc2tog over first 2 sts, sc in each of next 5 sts, 2 sc in last st, turn—8 sc.

Row 11: Ch 1, 2 sc in first sc, sc in each of next 5 sts, sc2tog over last 2 sts, do not turn—8 sc.

SKILL LEVEL
Easy

MATERIALS & TOOLS
4 colors of yarn: Drum color (A), rim color (B), drum top color (C), drumsticks color (D)

Crochet hook: Appropriate size hook to achieve a firm gauge with selected yarn

Tapestry needle

ABBREVIATIONS
Find instructions on page 17 for: sc2tog

FOR THESE DRUMS WE USED

Classic Elite Yarns Woodland (65% wool, 35% nettles; 1¾oz/50g = 131yd/100m) DK weight yarn (9): #3154 Red Grape (A), #3150 Sunshine (B), #3101 Ivory (C).

GAUGE CIRCLE
(see page 7) = 1"/2.5cm worked on 4.00mm (size G-6 U.S.) hook

FINISHED MEASUREMENT
2¼"/5.7cm wide x 3"/7.6cm tall

Dale of Norway Falk (100% superwash wool; 1¾oz/50g = 116yd/106m) DK weight yarn (9): #4018 Red (A), #2427 Gold (B), #2611 Sand (C) and (D).

GAUGE CIRCLE
(see page 7) = 1"/2.5cm worked on 4.00mm (size G-6 U.S.) hook

FINISHED MEASUREMENT
2¼"/5.7cm wide x 3"/7.6cm tall

Row 12 (RS): Rotate piece to work along convex side of piece (bottom of drum), sc in each row of drum—11 sc. Fasten off A.

Row 13: With RS facing, join A with sc in top corner of drum, sc in each of next 4 rows, sc2tog over next 2 rows, sc in each of next 5 rows, do not turn—11 sts. Fasten off A.

Rim and Top

Row 14: With RS facing, join B with sc in first sc of Row 12, at bottom corner of drum, sc in each of next 10 sc. Fasten off B.

Row 15 (RS): Rotate drum to work across top, and working in FLO of Row 13, join B with sc in first st at top of drum, sc in each of next 10 sc. Fasten off B.

Row 16: With RS facing, working in BLO of Row 13 at top of drum, sk first sc, join C with sc in next st, working across top of drum, hdc in next st, dc in next st, htr in next st, tr in next st, htr in next st, dc in next st, hdc in next st, sc in next st, skip last sc. Fasten off C.

Row 17: With RS facing, join B with sc in BL of first sc in Row 15 (skipped in Row 16); sc in each of next 9 sts in Row 16, sc in BL of last sc in Row 15 (skipped in Row 16). Fasten off B, leaving a 12"/30cm sewing length.

Drumsticks (optional) (make 2)

With D, ch 9, sl st in 2nd ch from hook. Fasten off D. To strengthen drumsticks, weave ends along back of ch before sewing in place.

FINISHING

For drum, use yarn end at beg of Row 15 to tack first sc of Row 15 on top of first st of Row 17. Tack last st of Row 15 on top of last sc of Row 17. Weave in all ends except long end.

Study zigzag line on drum in photo. Thread long yarn end from Row 17 into tapestry needle, bring thread to front from under last st of Row 15, bring thread under front 2 vertical lps of 3rd sc of Row 14, take thread back to top of drum and under front 2 vertical lps center sc of Row 15, bring thread under front 2 vertical lps of 3rd sc from other end of Row 14, take thread to back by inserting needle below last sc of Row 15. Fasten off.

Block, adjust zigzag, then tack. Weave in end.

Sew drumsticks to drum if desired.

watering cans

Watering cans remind me of the many houseplants and flowers my mom has raised over the years. She can grow just about anything!

SKILL LEVEL
Intermediate

MATERIALS & TOOLS
1 color of yarn: Watering can color (A)

Crochet hook: Appropriate size hook to achieve a firm gauge with selected yarn

Tapestry needle

PATTERN NOTE
Read about tambour st on page 11.

ABBREVIATIONS
Find instructions on page 16 for:
dc2tog

FOR THESE WATERING CANS WE USED

Cascade 220 Sport (100% Peruvian Highland wool; 1.75oz/50g = 164yd/15m) light weight yarn (3): #2409 Palm or #7827 Goldenrod (A).

GAUGE CIRCLE
(see page 7) = ⅞"/2.3cm worked on 3.50mm (size E-4 U.S.) hook

FINISHED MEASUREMENT
3½"/8.9cm x 2"/5.1cm

Plymouth Yarn Company Plymouth Select Worsted Merino Superwash (100% superwash fine merino wool; 3.5oz/100g = 218yd/198m) medium weight yarn (4): #42 Plum (A).

GAUGE CIRCLE
(see page 7) = 1"/2.5cm worked on 5.00mm (size H-8 U.S.) hook

FINISHED MEASUREMENT
4¼"/10.8cm x 2¼"/5.7cm

INSTRUCTIONS

WATERING CAN
With A, ch 23.

Row 1: To make the head of the spout, sc in 3rd ch from hook, hdc in next ch, ch 4, sc in 3rd ch from hook, hdc in next ch, sl st in ch st at base of first hdc; to make spout, work down the original ch with sc in each of next 4 ch, hdc in each of next 4 ch, dc2tog over next 2 ch; for the body of the watering can, sk next ch, dc in each of next 3 ch, dc2tog over next 2 ch, dc in each of next 3 ch, turn.

Row 2: Ch 3 (counts as dc here and throughout), dc in each of next 2 sts, dc2tog over next 2 ch, dc in each of next 3 sts; to make the brace that connects to the spout, ch 4, sk next 4 sts, sl st in each of next 2 sts, turn.

Row 3: Ch 1, sl st in each of next 4 ch, sl st in first dc, ch 3 (counts as dc), dc in each of next 2 sts, dc2tog over next 2 ch, dc in next st, dc in top of ch-3 turning ch, turn.

Row 4: Ch 3, dc in each of next 4 dc, dc in top of ch-3 turning ch, turn.

Row 5: Ch 1, sk first dc, (sc, hdc) in next dc, dc in next st, ch 3, sk next 2 dc, sl st in top of ch-3 turning ch; to make handle, ch 19, sl st in 2nd ch from hook, sl st in each of next 9 ch, [sk next ch, sl st in next ch] 3 times, sl st in each of next 2 ch, sl st in top of ch-3 turning ch (this st already has a sl st in it). Handle is not attached at the bottom.

Row 6: Work tambour st down side of watering can, ch 1 at corner, work tambour st across bottom to skipped st of foundation ch, ch 1 at corner, rotate piece to work tambour st up the other side of the watering can to top of Row 4 (excluding the brace and spout), cut yarn and needle-join to first sc of Row 5.

WATERING CAN THAT POURS IN THE OTHER DIRECTION
With A, ch 13.

Row 1: To make the head of the spout, sc in 3rd ch from hook, hdc in next ch, ch 4, sc in 3rd ch from hook, hdc in next ch, sl st in ch st at base of first hdc; to make spout, work down original ch with sc in each of next 4 ch, hdc in each of next 4 ch, 2 dc in next ch; for the body of the watering can, ch 11, dc in 4th ch from hook, dc in next ch, working along ch, dc2tog over next 2 ch, dc in each of next 3 ch, sk next ch, join with sl st to ch at base of last dc of spout, ch 7, working over foundation ch of spout, sk next 4 ch sts of spout, sl st in each of next 2 ch, turn.

Row 2: To finish the brace that connects the body of the watering can to the spout, ch 1, sl st in each of next 5 ch, sk 2 ch sts, dc in each of next 2 dc of Row 1, dc2tog over next 2 sts, dc in each of next 3 sts, turn.

Row 3: Ch 3 (counts as dc here and throughout), dc in each of next 2 sts, dc2tog over next 2 sts, dc in next st, dc in last sl st of brace from Row 2, turn.

Row 4: Ch 3, dc in each of next 4 dc, dc in top of ch-3 turning ch, turn.

Row 5: Ch 3, sk first 2 dc, dc in next st, (hdc, sc) in next dc, ch 1, sk next st, sl st in top of ch-3 turning ch.

Row 6: Work tambour st down side of watering can (excluding the brace and spout), ch 1 at corner, work tambour st across lower edge; to make handle, ch 19, sl st in 2nd ch from hook, sl st in next 2 ch, [sk next ch, sl st in next ch] 3 times, sl st in each of next 9 ch; continuing up the other side of watering can, work tambour st to top of Row 4. Handle is not attached at bottom.

FINISHING
Use closest yarn end to tack free end of handle to bottom or top corner of watering can. Weave in ends. Block.

kite

Flying kites is a favorite pastime of people all over the world, but kites are also used to fish, surf, landboard, and glide across the snow, as well as in military operations. I guess that means that the kite qualifies nicely as a toy, a tool, or as transportation!

SKILL LEVEL
Easy

MATERIALS & TOOLS
2 colors of yarn as desired: Kite color (A), kite stick and tail color (B)

Crochet hook: Appropriate size hook to achieve a firm gauge with selected yarn

Tapestry needle

PATTERN NOTE
Read about tambour st on page 11.

ABBREVIATIONS
Find instructions on pages 16 and 17 for: sc2tog, FLO

INSTRUCTIONS

KITE

Using A, ch 2.

Row 1: Sc in 2nd ch from hook, turn—1 sc.

Row 2: Ch 1, 3 sc in next sc, turn—3 sc.

Row 3: Ch 1, sc in each sc across, turn—3 sc.

Row 4: Ch 1, 2 sc in first sc, sc in each sc across to last sc, 2 sc in last sc, turn—5 sc.

Row 5: Ch 1, sc in each sc across, turn—5 sc.

Rows 6–11: Repeat Rows 4 and 5 three times—11 sc at end of last row.

Row 12: Working in FLO, ch 1, sk first sc, sc in each sc across to last 2 sts, sc2tog over last 2 sts, turn—9 sc.

Rows 13–15: Ch 1, sk first sc, sc in each sc across to last 2 sts, sc2tog over last 2 sts, turn—3 sc at end of last row.

Row 16: Ch 1, sk first sc, sc2tog over next 2 sts; if you want to outline the kite with tambour st, open the final lp wide and thread the ball of yarn through the lp to fasten off, but do not cut yarn. If you want to leave the kite's edges as they are, fasten off A.

Kite Sticks and Tail

Find the line of lps created by working in the FLO in Row 12. This line crosses the widest point of the kite. Begin with a lp of B on the hook. Work a row of tambour sts across the kite, along the line of lps, fasten off at the other end.

With a lp of B on the hook, begin at the top point of the kite, where A is still attached. Work a row of tambour sts down the middle of the length of the kite, making 1 st for each row of sc. At the lower point of the kite, continue as follows to create the kite's tail.

Tail: *Ch 6, (slst-picot) twice, sl st around the chain before the first picot of this pair, rotate the work toward the hook end of your hook, so that when you make the next ch st, it will go between the 2 picots; rep from * twice, ch 8. Fasten off.

FINISHING

Tambour st outline: With A, which is still attached at the top of the kite, work a line of tambour sts along the short edge of the kite, working 1 tambour st per row. At the corner, ch 1, continue working tambour sts down long edge of the kite. Work a tambour st into the bottom tip of the kite, ch 1, work another tambour st into the same corner. Tambour st up the other long edge of the kite, ch 1 at corner, continue tambour st up the short edge of the kite, at the top of the kite, ch 1, cut yarn and needle-join to first tambour st.

Weave in ends and block.

FOR THESE KITES WE USED

Skacel Collection Schulana Merino-Cotton 135 (53% merino wool, 47% cotton; 1.75oz/50g = 123yd/135m) DK weight yarn 🔢: #52 Pistachio (A), #31 Gold (B), and vice versa.

GAUGE CIRCLE
(see page 7) = ⅞"/2.2cm worked on 4.00mm (size G-6 U.S.) hook

FINISHED MEASUREMENT
2"/5.1cm wide x 3"/7.6cm tall, excluding tail

Cascade Ultra Pima Fine (100% pima cotton; 1.75oz/50g = 136.7yd/125m) sport weight yarn 🔢: #3767 coral (A), #3744 moss (B).

GAUGE CIRCLE
(see page 7) = ¾"/1.8cm worked on 3.50mm (size E-4 U.S.) hook

FINISHED MEASUREMENT
1¾"/4.4cm wide x 2½"/6.4cm tall, excluding tail

guitar

The idea of a camping vacation made me think of singing around the campfire. But why wait? Singing is lovely all year-round, especially with guitar accompaniment.

SKILL LEVEL
Easy

MATERIALS & TOOLS
4 colors of yarn: Sound hole color (A), rosette color (B), guitar body color (C), neck and head color (D)

Crochet hook: Appropriate size hook to achieve a firm gauge with selected yarn

Tapestry needle

ABBREVIATIONS
Find instructions on pages 16 and 17 for: sc2tog, htr

INSTRUCTIONS

GUITAR

With A, ch 4, join with sl st to form ring.

Rnd 1: Ch 2 (counts as hdc here and throughout), 9 hdc in ring; join with sl st in top of beg ch-2 and fasten off OR cut yarn and needle-join to first st of rnd—10 hdc.

Rnd 2: With RS facing, working in BLO, join B with sc in any st of Rnd 1, 2 sc in each of next 9 sts; join with sl st to first sc and fasten off OR cut yarn and needle-join to first st of rnd—19 sc.

Rnd 3: With RS facing, working in BLO, join C with hdc in first st of Rnd 2, 2 hdc in next st, hdc in next st, 2 hdc in next st, (hdc, sc) in next st, sc in each of next 2 sts, (sc, hdc) in next st, (dc, htr) in next st, 2 tr in each of next 2 sts, (htr, dc) in next st, (hdc, sc) in next st, sc in each of next 2 sts, (sc, hdc) in next st, 2 hdc in next st, hdc in next st, 2 hdc in next st, join with sl st in first hdc.

Rnd 4: Ch 2, hdc in each of next 3 hdc, 2 hdc in each of next 2 hdc, (hdc, sc) in next hdc, sc in next sc, sc2tog over next 2 sts, sc in next sc, (hdc, dc) in next hdc, (htr, tr) in next dc, *2 tr in next st, tr in next st, 2 tr in next st; rep from * once, (tr, htr) in next dc, (dc, hdc) in next hdc, sc in next sc, sc2tog over next 2 sts, sc in next sc, (sc, hdc) in next st, 2 hdc in each of next 2 hdc, hdc in each of next 3 hdc, join with sl st in top of beg ch-2.

Rnd 5: Ch 2, hdc in each of next 3 hdc, 2 hdc in next hdc, hdc in next hdc, 2 hdc in next hdc, 2 sc in next hdc, sl st in each of next 6 sts, sc in next dc, (sc, hdc) in next htr, (dc, htr) in next tr, (htr, tr) in next tr, tr

in next tr, *2 tr in next st, tr in next st, 2 tr in next st; rep from * once, tr in next tr, (tr, htr) in next tr, (htr, dc) in next tr, (hdc, sc) in next htr, sc in next dc, sl st in each of next 6 sts, 2 sc in next hdc, 2 hdc in next hdc, hdc in next hdc, 2 hdc in next hdc, hdc in each of next 3 sts, sl st in top of beg ch-2. Fasten off C.

Neck and Head

With D, ch 25.

Row 1: Dc in 4th ch from hook (this creates a ch-3 turning lp), working along chain, dc in each of next 3 ch, PM in dc you just finished, hdc in each of next 7 ch, dc in each of next 11 ch. Fasten off D, leaving a long sewing length.

Row 2: With RS facing, draw up lp of D at base of dc with marker, ch 1, sl st in same ch, [(sl st, ch 1, sl st) in next ch] twice, sl st in next ch, ch 2, sl st in each of next 3 ch of turning lp, ch 2, sl st in next dc, [(sl st, ch 1, sl st) in next ch] 3 times, ending in st with marker, remove marker. Fasten off D.

Bridge

With D, ch 8, sl st in 2nd ch from hook, sl st in each ch across. Fasten off D, leaving a long sewing length.

FINISHING

Sew neck and bridge to front of guitar using photo as a guide for placement. Weave in ends. Block.

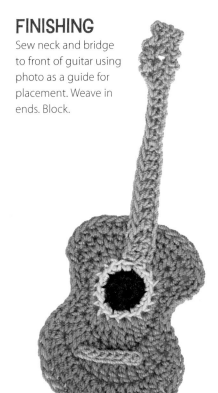

vacation transportation

I like to leave the vacation driving to someone else so I can indulge in cross-country crochet. Just think how much a person could crochet on a trip to Mars!

SKILL LEVEL
Easy

MATERIALS & TOOLS
Airplane: 1 color of yarn (A)

Automobile: 3 colors of yarn: car color (A), hubcap color (B), tire color (C)

Rocket ship: 5 colors of yarn: ship color (A), fin and porthole color (B), tailpipe color (C), flame colors (D) and (E)

Crochet hook: Appropriate size hook to achieve a firm gauge with selected yarn

Tapestry needle

PATTERN NOTES
For the rocket, htr-htr-trtog: [Yo (twice), draw up a lp in next ch, yo, draw through 2 lps] twice (for 2 htr-sts), yo (twice), draw up a lp in next ch, [yo, draw through 2 lps on hook] twice (for tr); (6 lps on hook), yo and draw through all lps on hook.

ABBREVIATIONS
Find instructions on pages 16 and 17 for: hdc2tog, tr2tog, htr

AIRPLANE

With A, ch 23.

Row 1: Hdc in 3rd ch from hook, hdc in each of next 17 ch, sc in next st, sk next ch, sl st in last ch, turn.

Row 2: Ch 1, sk next sc, sl st in each of next 2 hdc, sc in next st, hdc in each of next 15 sts, hdc in top of ch-2 turning ch, turn.

Row 3: Ch 2 (counts as hdc here and throughout), hdc in first st, hdc in each of next 3 sts, [ch 1, sk next st, hdc in next st]

5 times, hdc in each of next 2 sts, ch 2, sk next 2 sts, hdc in next st, turn.

Row 4: Ch 1, sk next hdc, sl st in first ch of next ch-2 sp, sc in next ch, hdc in each of next 16 sts or ch-1 spaces, hdc in top of ch-2 turning ch, turn.

Row 5: Ch 2, hdc in first st, hdc in next st, hdc2tog over next 2 sts, turn.

Row 6: Ch 2, hdc2tog in first 2 sts, hdc in next st, hdc in top of ch-2 turning ch. Fasten off A.

Front Wing

With A, leaving a long sewing length, ch 10.

Row 1: Sc in 2nd ch from hook, hdc in each of next 7 ch, 2 hdc in last ch, turn.

Row 2: Ch 3, dc in first st, hdc in each of next 7 sts, cut yarn and needle-join to next st OR sl st in next st and fasten off (1 st remains unworked). This end is the wing tip.

FOR THESE VEHICLES WE USED

Dale of Norway Dale Lille Lerke (53% merino wool, 47% cotton; 1¾oz/50g = 154yd/142m) DK weight yarn (3): (for airplane) #6621 pale blue (A).

GAUGE CIRCLE
(see page 7) = ¹³⁄₁₆"/2.1cm worked on 4.00mm (size G-6 U.S.) hook

FINISHED MEASUREMENT
4¼"/10.8 wide x 3⅝"/8.6cm tall for Airplane

Lion Brand LB Collection Angora Merino (80% extra-fine merino wool, 20% angora; 1.75oz/50g = 131yd/120m) light weight yarn (3): (for airplane) #108 Blue Bonnet (A).

GAUGE CIRCLE
(see page 7) = ⅞"/2.2cm worked on 4.00mm (size G-6 U.S.) hook

FINISHED MEASUREMENT
4⅜"/11.1 wide x 3¼"/8.3cm tall for Airplane

Dale of Norway Falk (100% superwash wool; 1¾oz/50g = 116yd/106m) DK weight yarn (3): (for automobile) #5646 Electric Blue (A), #0017 Off-White (B), #0090 Black (C); (for rocket ship) #4415 Pink (A), #4536 Magenta (B), #2417 Dandelion (C), #3309 Orange (D).

GAUGE CIRCLE
(see page 7) = 1"/2.5cm worked on 4.00mm (size G-6 U.S.) hook

FINISHED MEASUREMENT
4"/10.2 cm wide x 2½"/6.4cm tall for Automobile; 3"/7.6 cm wide x 5"/12.7cm tall for Rocket Ship

Cascade 220 Sport (100% Peruvian Highland wool; 1.75oz/50g = 164yd/15m) light weight yarn (3): (for automobile) #8895 Christmas Red (A), #8505 White (B), #8555 Black (C).

GAUGE CIRCLE
(see page 7) = ⅞"/2.2cm worked on 3.50mm (size E-4 U.S.) hook

FINISHED MEASUREMENT
3⅜"/9.2 wide x 2¼"/5.7cm tall for Automobile

Berroco Ultra® Alpaca Light (50% superfine alpaca, 50% Peruvian wool; 1.75oz/50g = 144yd/133m) sport weight yarn (2): (for rocket ship) #4201 Winter White (A), #42104 Peacock (B), #4217 Tupelo (C), #4234 Cardinal (D).

GAUGE CIRCLE
(see page 7) = ⅞"/2.2cm worked on 3.75mm (size F-5 U.S.) hook

FINISHED MEASUREMENT
2½"/6.4cm wide x 4¾"/12.1cm for Rocket Ship

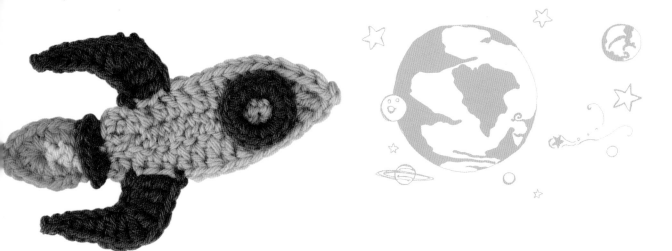

Back Wing

With A, leaving a long sewing length, ch 8.

Row 1: Sc in 2nd ch from hook, hdc in each of next 5 ch, 2 hdc in last ch, turn.

Row 2: Ch 3 (counts as dc), dc in first st, hdc in each of next 5 sts, cut yarn and needle-join to next st OR sl st in next st and fasten off (1 st remains unworked). This end is the wing tip.

FINISHING

Using long yarn ends, sew front wing to plane body, under 2nd and 3rd windows, as shown in photo. Sew back wing to back of body, above the same windows, so it doesn't show through windows. For a plane flying in the other direction, flip pieces around and sew front wing to front, back wing to back.

AUTOMOBILE

With A, ch 5, join with sl st to form ring.

Row 1: Ch 4 (counts as tr), (htr, dc, 4 hdc, dc, htr, tr) in ring, turn—10 sts.

Row 2: Ch 3 (counts as dc here and throughout), dc in first st, 2 dc in each of next 2 sts, 2 hdc in next st, hdc in each of next 2 sts, 2 hdc in next st, 2 dc in each of next 2 sts, 2 dc in top of ch-4 turning ch, turn—18 sts.

Row 3: Ch 3, dc in next st, 2 dc in next st, dc in next st, hdc in each of next 10 sts, dc in next st, 2 dc in next st, dc in next st, dc in top of ch-3 turning ch, turn—20 sts.

FOR AUTOMOBILE GOING ONE WAY

One way Row 4: Ch 2 (counts as hdc), hdc in first st, hdc in next 2 sts, 2 hdc in next st, hdc in next st, sl st in next st, ch 5, sk next 2 sts, dc in next st, ch 8, sk next 3 sts, sl st in next st, sc in next st, hdc in each of next 2 sts, 2 hdc in next st, hdc in next st, 2 hdc in next st, hdc in top of ch-3 turning ch, turn.

One way Row 5 (RS): Ch 2, hdc in first st, ch 1, sl st in each of next 8 sts, sk next sl-st, sl st in each of next 4 ch, ch 1, sc in next 4 ch, sc in next dc, sl st in each of next 5 ch, sl st in each of next 6 sts, ch 1, (hdc, ch 2, sl st) in top of ch-2 turning ch. Fasten off A.

FOR AUTOMOBILE GOING THE OTHER WAY

Other way Row 4: Ch 2 (counts as hdc), *2 hdc in next st, hdc in next st; rep from * once, hdc in next st, sc in next st, sl st in next st, ch 8, sk next 3 sts, dc in next st, ch 5, sk next 2 sts, sl st in next st, hdc in next st, 2 hdc in next st, hdc in each of next 2 sts, 2 hdc in top of ch-3 turning ch, turn.

Other way Row 5 (RS): Ch 2, hdc in first st, ch 1, sl st in each of next 6 sts, sl st in each of next 5 ch, sc in next dc, sc in each of next 4 ch, ch 1, sl st in each of next 4 ch, sk next sl-st, sl st in next sc, sl st in each of next 7 hdc, ch 1, (hdc, ch 2, sl st) in top of ch-2 turning ch. Fasten off A.

Tire and Fender (make 2)

Instructions are written with sl-st joins for Rnds 1 and 2, but for best results, needle-join these rnds.

With B, ch 5, join with sl st to form ring.

Rnd 1: Ch 1, 8 sc in ring, join with sl st in first sc—8 sts. Fasten off B.

Rnd 2: With RS facing, join C with 2 sc in any st of Rnd 1, 2 sc in each st around, join with sl st in first sc—16 sts. Fasten off C.

Rnd 3: With RS facing, working in BLO, join A with sl st in any st of Rnd 2, ch 2, sc in same st, *2 sc in next st, sc in next st; rep from * twice, ch 2, sl st in same st as last sc. Fasten off A, leaving long sewing length.

FINISHING

Use long yarn ends to sew fenders and tires to automobile body, using photo as a guide for placement. Weave in remaining ends. Block.

ROCKET SHIP

With A, ch 14.

Row 1: Sc in 3rd ch from hook (forms a ch-2 lp), hdc in next ch, dc in each of next 8 ch, hdc in each of next 2 ch, turn—14 sts.

Row 2: Ch 2 (counts as hdc), hdc in each of next 3 sts, dc in each of next 2 sts, htr in each of next 3 sts, (htr, dc) in next dc, 2 dc in next hdc, htr in next sc, (tr, ch 2, sl st in 2nd ch from hook, tr) in ch-2 lp at nose of rocket; rotate piece to work across opposite side of foundation ch, (htr, dc) in next ch (at base of sc), 2 dc in next ch, (dc, htr) in next ch, htr in each of next 3 ch, dc in next 2 ch, hdc in each of last 4 ch, ch 1, rotate piece to work along lower edge of rocket, work 5 sc, evenly spaced across lower edge, ch 1, sl st in top of ch-2 turning ch of Row 2, do not turn. Fasten off A.

First Fin

With RS facing, draw up lp of B in 2nd hdc of Row 2, ch 10, sl st in 2nd ch from hook, sc in next ch, hdc in each of next 3 ch, dc in next ch, (2 htr, tr) in next ch, 2 tr in next ch, tr in last ch, sk next 2 sts of Row 2, sl st in next st of Row 2. Fasten off B.

Second Fin

With RS facing, draw up lp of B in 5th st from end of Row 2 (it is the last dc of Row 2) on other side of rocket, ch 13, sl st in 2nd ch from hook, sc in next ch, hdc in each of next 3 ch, dc in next ch, htr-htr-trtog over next 3 ch, tr2tog over next 2 ch, tr in last ch, sk next 2 sts of Row 2, sl st in next st. Fasten off B.

Porthole

With B, ch 10, join with sl st to beg of ch to form ring.

Rnd 1: Draw up lp under ch-ring, ch 1, 15 sc in ring; leaving a long end for sewing, cut yarn and needle-join to first st of rnd OR join with sl st to first st of rnd, and, leaving a long end for sewing, fasten off B.

Tailpipe

With RS facing, join C with hdc in 2nd sc at bottom edge of rocket, 2 hdc in same st, 3 hdc in next sc. Fasten off C.

Flame

With D, ch 6.

Row 1: Hdc in 4th ch from hook (forms a ch-3 lp), dc in each of next 2 ch, do not turn. Fasten off D.

Row 2: Working across opposite side of foundation ch of Row 1, with RS facing, join E with sc in ch at base of last dc of Row 1, hdc in each of next 2 ch, (2 hdc, dc, slst-picot, dc, 2 hdc) in ch-3 lp at tip of flame, hdc in next hdc, hdc in next dc, sc in next dc. Fasten off E, leaving long sewing length.

FINISHING

Use yarn ends of fins to tack last tr of fin to side of rocket (this closes the gap and looks better). Sew porthole to front of rocket. Weave long end of flame across base of flame and pull to gather slightly, sew base of flame behind tailpipe as in photo. Weave in ends. Block.

little square book

Made in small thread, this book can be a dollhouse accessory. Or try it as a needle cozy! Illustrate a larger book with embroidery, beads, buttons, or crocheted motifs.

SKILL LEVEL
Easy

MATERIALS & TOOLS
3 colors of yarn: Paper color (A), book cover color (B), cover accent color (C)

Crochet hook: Appropriate size hook to achieve a firm gauge with selected yarn

Tapestry needle

Optional: Embroidery floss, beads, buttons, or crocheted motifs to illustrate book, with sewing needle and thread

INSTRUCTIONS

PAGES (MAKE 3)

With A, ch 4, sl st in first ch to form ring.

Rnd 1: Ch 2, 2 hdc in ring, ch 2, *3 hdc in ring, ch 2; rep from * twice, join with sl st in top of beg ch-2—12 hdc, 4 ch-2 sp.

Rnd 2: Ch 2, hdc in each of next 2 hdc, (2 hdc, ch 2, 2 hdc) in next ch-2 sp, *hdc in each of next 3 hdc, (2 hdc, ch 2, 2 hdc) in next ch-2 sp; rep from * twice, join with sl st to top of beg ch-2—28 hdc, 4 ch-2 sp. Fasten off A.

COVER (MAKE 2)

With A, ch 4, sl st in first ch to form ring.

Rnd 1: Ch 2, 2 hdc in ring, ch 2, *3 hdc in ring, ch 2; rep from * twice, join with sl st in top of beg ch-2—12 hdc, 4 ch-2 sp.

Rnd 2: Ch 3, dc in each of next 2 hdc, (2 dc, ch 2, 2 dc) in next ch-2 sp, *dc in each of next 3 hdc, (2 dc, ch 2, 2 dc) in next ch-2 sp; rep from * twice, join with sl st to top of beg ch-3—28 dc, 4 ch-2 sp. Fasten off A.

FINISHING

Weave in ends. Block pieces, pinning out corners to make angles sharp.

BIND BOOK

Place a sl knot of B on hook, hold one cover piece with RS facing, insert hook into ch-2 sp at corner; insert hook into ch-2 sp at one corner of each page; hold second cover piece with WS facing, insert hook into ch-2 sp of second cover piece, yo, and, letting yarn flow freely, pull through all covers and pages of book and lp on hook to complete sl st. Do not pull too tightly, because pages and covers should be close to their natural thickness.

*Insert hook in next hdc of each piece, yo, draw yarn through all layers and through lp on hook to complete next sl st; rep from * across for each rem hdc down edge of pages, insert hook into next ch-2 sp at corner of each piece, yo, pull through all layers and through lp on hook to complete next sl st. Fasten off B. Weave in ends.

SPINE

Row 1: With front cover facing, join B with sc in first ch-2 sp of front cover on spine side, sk first sl st of spine, sc in each of next 7 sl sts of spine, sk last sl st of spine, sc in next ch-2 sp of front cover, turn—9 sc.

Row 2: Ch 3 (counts as dc), dc in each sc across, turn—9 dc.

Row 3: Ch 1, sc in first dc, sc in each of next 7 dc, sc in top of turning ch—9 sc. Fasten off B, leaving a long sewing length.

Bend spine around to back of book, sew first sc to matching ch-2 lp of back cover, sew each following spine st to corresponding st of back cover until last st, sew last st of spine to ch-2 lp of back cover.

FINISHING

Weave in ends. Decorate book as desired.

FOR THESE BOOKS WE USED

Cascade 220 Sport (100% Peruvian Highland wool; 1.75oz/50g = 164yd/15m) light weight yarn (3): #8505 White (A), #7808 Purple Hyacinth (B).

GAUGE CIRCLE
(see page 7) = ⅞"/2.2cm worked on 3.50mm (size E-4 U.S.) hook

FINISHED MEASUREMENT
1¾"/4.4cm wide x 1⅝"/4.1cm tall x 1"/2.5cm deep

Lion Brand Kitchen Cotton (100% cotton; 2oz/57g = 99yd/90m) medium weight yarn (4): #98 Vanilla (A), #113 Hot Pepper (B).

GAUGE CIRCLE
(see page 7) = 1¼"/3.2cm worked on 5.00mm (size H-8 U.S.) hook

FINISHED MEASUREMENT
2¾"/7cm wide x 2½"/6.4cm tall x ¼"/3.2cm

home

dress-up time

I drew dresses like this in my childhood, inspired by fairy tales, no doubt. If it were easier to get in and out of a car wearing dresses like this, I would like to wear them in everyday life.

INSTRUCTIONS

SKIRT

With A, ch 7.

Row 1 (RS): 2 dc in 4th ch from hook, dc in each of next 2 ch, 3 dc in last ch, turn—8 dc (ch-3 lp counts as dc).

Row 2 (WS): Ch 3 (counts as dc here and throughout), dc in first dc, dc in next st, 2 dc in next st, dc in each of next 2 sts, 2 dc in next st, dc in next st, 2 dc in top of beg ch-3, turn—12 dc.

Row 3: Ch 3, dc in first dc, dc in each of next 5 sts, 2 dc in next st, dc in each of next 4 sts, 2 dc in top of beg ch-3, turn—15 dc.

Row 4: Sc-picot, working in BLO, sc in first dc, *sc-picot, sk next st, sc in next st; rep from * 5 times, sc-picot, (sc, sc-picot, sl st) in top of beg ch-3, turn—9 picots.

SKILL LEVEL
Intermediate

MATERIALS & TOOLS
3 colors of yarn: Dress color (A), ruffle and trim color (B), drape color (C)

Crochet hook: Appropriate size hook to achieve a firm gauge with selected yarn

Tapestry needle

ABBREVIATIONS
Find instructions on page 17 for: sc-picot

FOR THIS DRESS WE USED
Cascade Ultra Pima Fine (100% pima cotton; 1.75oz/50g = 136.7yd/125m) sport weight yarn (2): #3743 Yellow Rose (A), #3772 Cornflower (B), #3728 White (C).

GAUGE CIRCLE
(see page 7) = ¾"/1.9cm worked on 3.50mm (size E-4 U.S.) hook

FINISHED MEASUREMENT
4½"/11.4cm wide x 4"/10.2cm tall.

(Because you turned your work, the FLs of Row 3 are now BLs.)

Row 5: Ch 3, dc in first st, working behind sts of Row 4, in the rem BLO of Row 3, dc in each of next 13 sts, 2 dc in top of beg ch-3, turn—17 dc.

Rows 6 and 7: Ch 3, dc in each of next 15 sts, dc in top of beg ch-3, turn—17 dc.

Row 8 (WS): Sc-picot, working BLO, sc in first dc, *sc-picot, sk next st, sc in next st; rep from * 6 times, sc-picot, (sc, sc-picot, sl st) in top of beg ch-3, do not turn—10 picots. Fasten off A.

Row 9 (WS): With WS facing, working in FLO of sts in Row 7, join B with 2 tr in first st of Row 7 (it already has sts in it), 2 tr in FLO of each st across, 2 tr in top of beg ch-3, turn—34 tr.

Row 10: Ch 1, sl st in first st, *ch 1, sl st in next st; rep from * across, ch 1, sl st in last st again. Fasten off B.

TOP

Row 1: At top of skirt, with RS facing, working across opposite side of foundation ch, join A with hdc in first ch, hdc in each of next 2 ch, 2 hdc in last ch, turn—5 hdc.

Row 2: Ch 2 (counts as hdc here and throughout), hdc in first st, hdc in each of next 3 sts, 2 hdc in last st, turn—7 hdc.

Row 3: Ch 2, hdc in each of next 5 sts, hdc in top of beg ch-2, turn—7 hdc.

Row 4:
Cap sleeve
Ch 5, sl st in 2nd ch from hook, ch 3, sl st in 2nd ch from hook, sk next 2 picots, hdc in next ch, hdc2tog over next 2 ch;

Scoop neck
Hdc in each of next 2 hdc of Row 3, sc in each of next 3 sts, hdc in next st, hdc in top beg ch-2, PM in top of ch 2 where hdc already is;

Other cap sleeve
Ch 4, sl st in 2nd ch from hook, ch 3, sl st in 2nd ch from hook, sk next 2 picots, hdc in next ch, 2 hdc in next ch, going down side of dress top, sk side of hdc at end of scoop neck, sl st to top of st with marker, remove marker. Fasten off A.

DRAPE FOR SKIRT (MAKE 2)
With C, ch 14.

Row 1 (RS): Sc in 2nd ch from hook (this creates a ch-1 lp at lower tip of drape), hdc in next ch, dc in each of next 2 ch, htr in each of next 4 ch, dc in each of next 2 ch, hdc in next ch, sc in next ch, ch 1, sl st in last ch, do not turn.

Row 2 (RS): Rotate piece to work across opposite side of foundation ch, ch 1, sc in next ch (this should be the one with an sc in it already), hdc in next ch, dc in each of next 2 ch, htr in each of next 4 ch, dc in each of next 2 ch, hdc in next ch, sc in next ch ch 1, sl st in ch-1 lp at lower tip. Fasten off B, leaving long sewing length. This is the lower tip of drape.

Trim for one drape (RS)
Join B with sl st in ch-1 at top of drape, *ch 1, sl st in next st; rep from * across bottom tip of drape. Fasten off B.

Trim for other drape (RS)
Join B with sl st in last ch at lower tip of drape, *ch 1, sl st in next st; rep from * across to top of drape. Fasten off B.

CORSAGE
With C, leaving a 4"/10.2cm yarn end, wrap yarn around your finger to create a lp, insert hook into thread lp and draw up a lp, (ch 3, sl st into thread lp) 5 times. Fasten off, leaving another long sewing length, pull first yarn end to tighten lp and close the center of the flower.

FINISHING
Weave in ends except long ends for sewing. Block pieces, avoiding ruffle at bottom edge of skirt. Sew drapes to skirt as in photo, with trim sides facing each other. Sew corsage to top as in photo. Weave in rem ends.

wellies

Need a rain puddle emptied? Dress the nearest child in a raincoat and Wellington boots, and the job is as good as done. You'll be tempted to put on your own boots and join the fun.

SKILL LEVEL
Intermediate

MATERIALS & TOOLS
1 or 2 colors of yarn: Boot color (A), trim color (B)

Crochet hook: Appropriate size hook to achieve a firm gauge with selected yarn

Tapestry needle

PATTERN NOTE
Either side of boot can be RS.

ABBREVIATIONS
Find instructions on pages 16 and 17 for: joined-tr, htr

INSTRUCTIONS

BOOT (MAKE 2)

Using A, ch 16.

Row 1: Sc in 3rd ch from hook (this forms a ch-2 loop at the tip of the toe), hdc in each of next 2 ch, 2 dc in next ch, dc in next ch, 2 dc in next ch, dc in next ch, tr in each of rem 7 ch, turn—16 sts.

Row 2: Ch 4 (counts as first tr), joined-tr in next st, tr in each of next 4 sts, dc in each of next 4 sts, (dc, 3 htr, dc) in next st, hdc in each of next 3 sts, sc in each of next 2 sts, sl st in top of turning ch. Fasten off A. The second htr of the 5 sts that are clustered together at the heel of the boot is the center st of the heel—21 sts plus sl st at end.

Top Trim and Tread for Left-Facing Boot

Top trim: Holding the boot at the top, so that the toe points to the left, join B with sl st at top corner of boot (the heel should be below), ch 7, sl st in 5th ch from hook; working across the top of the boot, work 6 hdc, evenly spaced across, working last hdc in the other top corner of the boot. Fasten off.

Tread: Holding the boot with the sole side up, with toe to the right, join B with sl st in the final sl st of Row 2 of boot, ch 1, [ch 2, sl st in 2nd ch from hook, sc in next st] 4 times, sl st in next st, [sc in next st, ch 2, sl st in 2nd ch from hook] twice, ch 1, sl st in next st (center st of the heel). Fasten off.

Top Trim and Tread for Right-Facing Boot

Top Trim: Holding the boot at the top, so that the toe points to the right, join B with hdc at top corner of boot (the toe should be below), working across the top of the boot, work 5 more hdc, evenly spaced across, ending with last hdc 1 st-width away from other top corner of the boot. Ch 5, sl st in 5th ch from hook, ch 2, sl st at top corner of boot. Fasten off.

Tread: Holding the boot with the sole side up and with toe to the left, join B with sl st in the center st of the heel, ch 1, [ch 2, sl st in 2nd ch from hook, sc in next st] twice, sl st in next st, [sc in next st, ch 2, sl st in 2nd ch from hook] 4 times, ch 1, sl st in final sl st of Row 2 of boot. Fasten off.

FINISHING

Weave in ends and block.

FOR THESE BOOTS WE USED

Dale of Norway Falk (100% superwash wool; 1¾oz/50g = 116yd/106m) DK weight yarn (3): #8817 Lime, #3609 Poppy, or #5624 Blue Bell (A), #8246 Kelly Green, #4018 Red, or #5646 Electric Blue (B).

GAUGE CIRCLE
(see page 7) = 1"/2.5cm worked on 4.00mm (size G-6 U.S.) hook

FINISHED MEASUREMENT
2"/5.1cm x 3⅜"/8.6cm

home

vintage TV

Time was, when you had to walk over to the television to change the channels. No, really—it's true! We called the TV-top antenna "rabbit ears," which is entirely possible to portray in crochet.

INSTRUCTIONS

TV

With A, ch 8.

Rnd 1: Hdc in 4th ch from hook, hdc in next 3 ch, ch 2, sl st in last ch—4 hdc with ch-lps at ends.

Rnd 2: Ch 2 (counts as first hdc here and throughout), working across opposite side of foundation ch, hdc in next ch, dc in each of next 2 ch, hdc in next ch, 3 hdc in next ch, dc in next ch, 3 hdc in next ch, hdc in next hdc, dc in each of next 2 sts, hdc in next st, 3 hdc in next ch, dc in next ch, 2 hdc in same st as ch-2 at beg of rnd, join with sl st to top of beg ch-2—22 sts.

Rnd 3: Ch 2, hdc in each of next 5 sts, 3 hdc in next hdc (this should be the center st of the first corner), hdc in each of next 3 sts, 3 hdc in next hdc, hdc in each of next 6 sts, 3 hdc in next hdc, hdc in each of next 3 sts, 3 hdc in next hdc, join with sl st to top of beg ch-2—28 sts. Fasten off. Weave in ends. TV tube finished.

Rnd 4: All corners of this rnd are worked in 3rd st of 3-hdc-corners of prev rnd. Working in BLO around, join B with 3 hdc in last hdc of prev rnd for corner, *sc in each of next 2 sts, sl st in each of next 4 sts, sc in each of next 2 sts, 3 hdc in next st for corner, sc in each of next 2 sts, sl st in next st, sc in each of next 2 sts*, 3 hdc in next st for corner; rep from * to * once, join with sl st to first hdc of rnd—38 sts. Fasten off B, leaving a long sewing length. With sewing length, embroider a "reflection" in the nearest corner of the TV tube, as shown in photo. Weave in ends.

Rnd 5: All corners in this rnd are worked in the middle st of 3-hdc-corners of prev rnd. Find the corner across the TV horizontally from the beg/end of Rnd 4 (bottom right-hand corner), working in BLO, join C with dc in the middle st of the 3-hdc in the corner, hdc in each of next 7 sts, (dc, ch 2, sc) in next corner st, sl st in each of next 10 sts, (sc, ch 1, sc) in next corner st, sl st in each of next 7 sts, (sc, ch 1, sc) in next corner st, sl st in each of next 10 sts, sc in next st (it already has a dc in it), ch 2, sl st in top of first dc of rnd—42 sts, 2 ch-1 sp, 2 ch-2 lp.

Work now progresses in a row. Only one side of the TV is worked in this row.

Row 6: Ch 3, dc in first dc of prev rnd, dc in each of next 8 sts, ch 3, sl st in next ch—9 dc, 2 ch-3 lps. Fasten off C, leaving a long sewing length.

Work now progresses in a rnd.

Rnd 7: Working in BLO around, join D with (sc, ch 1, sc) in 3rd ch of beg ch-3 lp of Row 6, sc in each of next 9 dc, (sc, ch 1, sc) in next ch, sc in each of next 2 ch, sc in next sl st, sc in next ch, sc in each of next 12 sts, (sc, ch 1, sc) in next ch, sc in each of next 9 sts, (sc, ch 1, sc) in next ch, working along bottom edge of TV, sc in each of next 12 sts, sc in each of next 2 ch, sk sl st, sc in each of next 2 ch, join with sl st to first sc of rnd and fasten off D OR cut yarn and needle-join to first sc of rnd—58 sc, 4 ch-1 sp.

Pedestal
Looking at bottom edge of TV and working in BLO across, with C, draw up lp in 3rd st past ch-1 sp at corner, sc in next st, hdc in each of next 10 sts, sc in next st, sl st in next st. Fasten off C.

Antenna
Looking at top edge of TV, join D with sc in 8th st past ch-1 sp at corner, hdc in next st, [ch 9, sc in 2nd ch from hook, sl st in each of next 7 ch] twice, sl st in first ch of first antenna, hdc in next st of TV, sc in next st. Fasten off D.

FOR THESE TVS WE USED

Berroco Ultra® Alpaca Light (50% super fine alpaca, 50% Peruvian wool; 1.75oz/50g = 144yd/133m) sport weight yarn (**2**): #42191 Azure Mix (A), #4201 Winter White (B), #4279 Potting Soil Mix (C), #4217 Tupelo (D).

GAUGE CIRCLE
(see page 7) = ⅞"/2.2cm worked on 3.75mm (size F-5 U.S.) hook

FINISHED MEASUREMENT
3¼"/8.3cm x 2½"/6.4cm excluding antenna

Classic Elite Yarns Liberty Wool (100% washable wool; 1¾oz/50g = 122yd/111m) DK/sport weight yarn (**3**): #7835 Citronella (A), #7816 Ecru (B), #7850 Gold (C), #7818 Fresh Clay (D).

GAUGE CIRCLE
(see page 7) = ⅞"/2.2cm worked on 4.00mm (size G-6 U.S.) hook

FINISHED MEASUREMENT
3⅝"/9.2cm x 2¾"/7cm

Dials
(make 2)

With D, ch 4, join with sl st to first ch to form ring.

Rnd 1: Ch 1, 6 sc in ring, leaving long end for sewing, cut yarn and needle-join to first sc of rnd.

Rabbit Ears (instead of regular antenna)
Looking at top edge of TV, join B or desired color with sc in 8th st to the left of top right-hand corner ch-1 sp, hdc in next st (first ear made), *ch 11, sl st in 3rd ch from hook, sl st in next ch, sc in each of next 5 ch, sl st in each of next 2 ch; rep from * once (second ear made), sl st in first ch of first ear, hdc in next st of Rnd 7, sc in next st. Fasten off.

FINISHING
Sew dials to C-color panel as shown in photo. Use long C sewing length to make a single st across each dial. Weave in ends. Block.

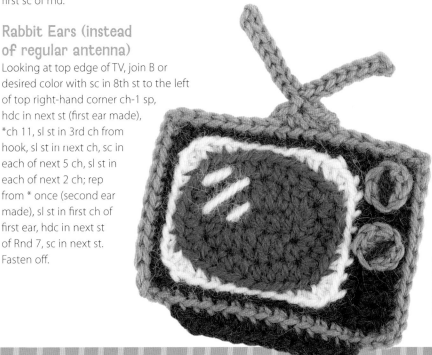

costumed kids

Kids love to dress up in costumes all year-round, so why not make these crocheted costumed creatures today for your favorite little princess or Martian?

INSTRUCTIONS

GHOST

With A, ch 13.

Row 1: Hdc in 3rd ch from hook (forms ch-2 lp), hdc in each of next 3 ch, dc in each of next 7 ch, turn—11 sts and ch-2 lp.

Row 2: Ch 3 (counts as dc here and throughout), dc in each of next 5 sts, hdc in each of next 4 sts, 2 hdc in next st, 3 hdc in each of next 2 ch of ch-2 lp, working across opposite side of foundation ch, 2 hdc in next ch, hdc in each of next 4 ch, dc in each of next 6 ch, turn—30 sts.

Row 3 (RS): Ch 3, dc in each of next 3 sts, hdc in each of next 4 sts, sc in each of next 4 sts, 2 sc in each of next 6 sts, sc in each of next 4 sts, hdc in each of next 4 sts, dc in each of last 4 sts—36 sts.

Edging row: With RS still facing, rotate to work along lower edge of ghost, where you will see the sides of 5 dc-sts (or ch-3 lps which count as dc), ch 2, sl st in side of next dc, (ch 3, sl st in side of next dc) 4 times, ch 2, sl st in top of ch-3 at beg of Row 3. Fasten off.

Eyes (make 2)

With B, ch 3, join with sl st to form ring. Fasten off, leaving a long sewing length.

First Shoe

Each shoe is made into 1 st on edging row. With RS of edging row facing, *join C with a sl st in middle st of 3rd ch lp, ch 2, sc in 2nd ch from hook, (2 hdc) in middle st of 3rd ch lp, ch 1, sl st in middle st of 3rd ch lp. Fasten off.*

Second Shoe

With WS facing, rep from * to * of first shoe.

FINISHING

Sew eyes in place. Weave in ends. Block. To make ghost in profile, crochet both shoes from the same side of ghost so they will point in same direction; sew on only one eye as pictured.

LITTLE WITCH

Head

With D, ch 4, join with sl st to form ring.

Rnd 1: Ch 2 (counts as hdc here and throughout), 11 hdc in ring, cut yarn with enough length for sewing and needle-join to first st of rnd—12 sts.

Hair

Join E with sl st in any st of head, ch 7, sl st in 2nd ch from hook, sl st in each ch across, sl st in same st of head as first sl st, ch 9, sl st in 2nd ch from hook, sl st in each ch across, sl st in same st of head as first sl st, sl st in next 4 sts (I will refer to 4th sl st in this group as "last sl st"), ch 9, sl st in 2nd ch from hook, sl st in each ch across,

sl st in same st of head as last sl st, ch 7, sl st in 2nd ch from hook, sl st in each ch across, sl st in same st of head as last sl st. Fasten off E. Use yarn ends to tame this crazy hair: tack the two strands together close to their roots, then tack them to the head if desired.

FOR THESE COSTUMES WE USED

Cascade 220 Sport (100% Peruvian Highland wool; 1.75oz/50g = 164yd/15m) light weight yarn (3): (for ghost) #8505 White (A), #9568 Twilight Blue (B); (for witch) #8555 Black (C) and (F), #8622 Camel (D) and (J), #2409 Palm (E), #7808 Purple Hyacinth (G), #8686 Brown (I).

GAUGE CIRCLE
(see page 7) = ⅞"/2.2cm worked on 3.50mm (size E-4 U.S.) hook

FINISHED MEASUREMENT
2"/5.1cm x 3¼"/8.3 for ghost; 3"/7.6cm x 3¾"/9.5cm for witch; 1"/2.5cm x 3"/7.6cm for broom

Dale of Norway Falk (100% superwash wool; 1¾oz/50g = 116yd/106m) DK weight yarn (3): (for princess) #3072 Cocoa (D), #0090 Black (E), #2427 Gold (F), #8817 Lime (G), #4516 Peony (K).

GAUGE CIRCLE
(see page 7) = 1"/2.5cm worked on 4.00mm (size G-6 U.S.) hook

FINISHED MEASUREMENT
3¼"/8.3cm x 4"/10.2cm for princess

Berroco Ultra® Alpaca Light (50% super fine alpaca, 50% Peruvian wool; 1.75oz/50g = 144yd/133m) sport weight yarn (2): (for Martian) #4217 Tupelo (C), #4275 Pea Soup Mix (D), #42104 Briny Deep (G), #4280 Mahogany Mix (H).

GAUGE CIRCLE
(see page 7) = ⅞"/2.2cm worked on 3.75mm (size F-5 U.S.) hook

FINISHED MEASUREMENT
3"/7.6cm x 4"/10.2cm for Martian

home

Hat

With F, ch 2.

Row 1: Sc in 2nd ch from hook, turn—1 sc.

Row 2: Ch 1, 2 sc in next sc, turn—2 sc.

Row 3: Ch 1, sc in each st across, turn—2 sc.

Row 4: Ch 1, sc in first st, 2 sc in next st, turn—3 sc.

Row 5: Ch 1, sc in each st across, turn—3 sc.

Row 6: Ch 1, 2 sc in first st, sc in each of next 2 sts, turn—4 sc.

Row 7: To make brim, ch 4, sc in 2nd ch from hook, sc in next 2 ch, sc each of next 4 sc (these are the sts of Row 6), ch 4, sc in 2nd ch from hook, sc in each of next 2 ch, join with sl st to side of hat at base of Row 6. Fasten off F, leaving a long sewing length.

Dress

With G, ch 18.

Row 1: Hdc in 4th ch from hook (ch-lp counts as first st), hdc in each of next 3 ch, [hdc2tog over next 2 ch] 3 times, hdc in each of next 4 ch, dc in next ch, turn—13 sts.

Row 2: Sl st in first 4 sts, (sl st, sc) in next st, hdc in next st, dc in next st, hdc in next st, sc in next st, turn, leaving rem sts unworked—5 sl sts, 5 sts for dress body.

Row 3: Ch 3 (counts as dc here and throughout), dc in first sc, dc in each of next 3 sts, 2 dc in last sc, turn—7 sts.

Row 4: Ch 3, dc in first st to complete inc, dc in each of next 5 sts, 2 dc in top of ch-3 turning ch, turn—9 sts.

Row 5: Ch 3, dc in each of next 7 sts, dc in turning ch of prev row, turn—9 sts.

Row 6: Ch 1, sc in first st, hdc in next st, dc in each of next 5 sts, hdc in next st, sc in last st. Fasten off G.

First Shoe

Each shoe is made into 1 st. With RS of Row 6 of dress facing, *join C with a sl st in 4th st of row, ch 2, sc in 2nd ch from hook, (2 hdc, ch 1, sl st) in 4th st of row. Fasten off.*

Second Shoe

With WS facing, rep from * to * of first shoe.

Hands

With RS facing, join D with a sl st in ch-3 lp at end of one sleeve, *ch 2, (hdc, ch 2, sl st) in same ch. Fasten off D.* For other hand, with RS facing, join D in side of dc at end of other sleeve, rep bet * and *.

FINISHING

Sew hat to head, covering sl sts at top of head, center head on Row 1 of dress as shown in photo and sew in place. Weave in ends. Block.

Broom

With I, ch 10.

Row 1: Sl st in 2nd ch from hook, sl st in each ch across. Fasten off I, leaving a long sewing length—11 sl sts.

With J, ch 3.

Row 1: (Hdc, ch 2, sl st) in 3rd ch from hook, turn.

Row 2: Ch 1, 2 sc in ch at base of hdc, turn—2 sc.

Row 3: Ch 5 to 7 sts, sl st in 2nd ch from hook, sl st in each ch across, sl st in first sc, [ch 5 to 7 sts, sl st in 2nd ch from hook, sl st in each ch across, sl st in second sc] twice. Fasten off J.

FINISHING

With long yarn end, sew broomstick to hdc at top of bristles, wrap yarn end around sc-row 2 or 3 times, then weave in end. Weave in remaining ends and block. Sew seed beads in place for eyes, embroider mouth.

LITTLE PRINCESS

Head

With D, ch 4, join with sl st to form ring.

Rnd 1: Ch 2 (counts as hdc here and throughout), 11 hdc in ring, cut yarn with enough length for sewing and needle-join to first st of rnd—12 sts.

Hair

With E, ch 12, 2 sc in 2nd ch from hook, 2 sc in each ch across, 2 sc in any st of head, [sc in next st, 2 sc in next st] twice, sc in next st, ch 12, 2 sc in 2nd ch from hook, 2 sc in each ch across. Fasten off E.

Crown

With F, slst-picot 3 times, ch 1, rotate piece so you can see base of picots, sl st in base of each picot across. Fasten off F, leaving a long sewing length.

Dress

With G, ch 18.

Row 1: Hdc in 4th ch from hook (ch-lp counts as first st), hdc in next 3 ch, [hdc2tog over next 2 ch] 3 times, hdc in each of next 4 ch, dc in next ch, turn—13 sts.

Row 2: Sl st in each of first 4 sts, (sl st, sc) in next st, hdc in next st, dc in next st, hdc in next st, sc in next st, turn, leaving rem sts unworked—5 sl sts, 5 sts for dress body.

Row 3: Ch 3 (counts as dc here and throughout), dc in first sc, dc in each of next 3 sts, 2 dc in last sc, turn—7 sts.

Row 4: Ch 3, dc in first st to complete inc, dc in each of next 5 sts, 2 dc in top of ch-3 turning ch, turn—9 sts.

Row 5: Ch 1, sc in first st, hdc in next st, dc in each of next 5 sts, hdc in next st, sc in last st, turn—9 sts. Fasten off G.

Row 6: Join K with sc in first st, sc in each of next 3 sts, 2 sc in next st, sc in each of last 4 sts, turn—10 sc. Fasten off K.

Row 7: Join G with sc in first st, sc in each of next 4 sts, 2 sc in next st, sc in each of last 4 sts, turn—11 sc. Fasten off G.

Row 8: Join K with a sl st in first st, *3 hdc in next st, sl st in next st; rep from * 4 times. Fasten off K.

Either side of dress can be right side.

Hands

With RS facing, join D with a sl st in ch-3 lp at end of one sleeve, *ch 2, (hdc, ch 2, sl st) in same ch. Fasten off D.* For other hand, with RS facing, join D in side of dc at end of other sleeve, rep bet * and *.

FINISHING

Use E yarn ends to tack first/last st of curls to side of head. Weave in ends except for sewing ends. Sew crown to hair as shown in photo. Sew head to top of dress as shown. Sew on beads for eyes and embroider a mouth.

LITTLE MARTIAN

Hold on a minute! Is this a costume? Or is it the real McCoy?

Head

With D, ch 4, join with sl st to first ch-st to form ring.

Rnd 1: Ch 2 (counts as hdc), 11 hdc in ring, join with sl st to top of ch-2 at beg of rnd—12 sts.

Rnd 2 (antennae): *Ch 6, (2 hdc, ch 2, sl st) in 3rd ch from hook, sl st in each of next 3 ch, sl st in same st of head,* sl st in next st; rep from * to * once. Fasten off D.

Shirt

With G, ch 18.

Row 1: Hdc in 4th ch from hook (ch-lp counts as first st), hdc in each of next 3 ch, [hdc2tog over next 2 ch] 3 times, hdc in each of next 4 ch, dc in next ch, turn—13 sts.

Row 2: Sl st in first 4 sts, (sl st, sc) in next st, hdc in next st, dc in next st, hdc in next st, sc in next st, turn, leaving rem sts unworked—5 sl sts, 5 sts for dress body.

Row 3: Ch 3 (counts as dc), dc in first sc, dc in each of next 3 sts, 2 dc in last sc, turn—7 sts.

Row 4: Ch 2 (counts as hdc), hdc in next st, dc in each of next 3 sts, hdc in next st, hdc in top of ch-3 turning-ch—7 sts. Fasten off G.

Hands

With RS facing, join D with a sl st in ch-3 lp at end of one sleeve, *ch 2, (hdc, ch 2, sl st) in same ch. Fasten off D.* For other hand, with RS facing, join D in side of dc at end of other sleeve, rep bet * and *.

Trousers

With RS facing, join H with a sl st in 2nd st of Row 4 of shirt, *ch 7, dc in 4th ch from hook, dc in each of next 3 ch, sk 1 st of shirt, sl st in next st; rep from * for second trouser leg. Fasten off H. Use one yarn end to sew top edge of trousers to bottom edge of shirt, and sew the top st of the legs together.

First Shoe

Each shoe is made into 1 st. With RS facing, join C with a sl st in 2nd ch of ch-3 lp on front-right trouser leg, *ch 2, sc in 2nd ch from hook, (2 hdc, ch 1, sl st) in 2nd ch of trouser leg. Fasten off.*

Second Shoe

With WS facing, join C with a sl st in 2nd ch of ch-3 lp on other trouser leg, rep from * to * of first shoe.

FINISHING

Sew head to top of shirt as shown. Weave in ends and block. Sew on beads for eyes and embroider a mouth.

MARTIAN IN DISGUISE?

Martians love Halloween; it allows them to roam undetected among Earthlings, plus they get free candy! Little Zek was warned not to stay out too late or eat too much chocolate this year, but he seems to have already forgotten.

cozy home

Build your custom crocheted home in less than one day! Choose from several attractive crocheted features. The price is right, but you'll have to be very small and two dimensional to live there.

SKILL LEVEL
Intermediate

MATERIALS & TOOLS
3 or more colors of yarn: wall color (A), roof color (B), door color (C), small amounts of other colors as needed for embellishment

Crochet Hook: Appropriate size hook to achieve a firm gauge with selected yarn

Tapestry needle

Optional: Embroidery floss or beads to decorate house

PATTERN NOTE
Read about tambour st on page 11.

ABBREVIATIONS
Find instructions on pages 16 and 17 for: BL, BLO, FPhdc, RS, sc3tog, slst-picot, WS

home

INSTRUCTIONS

WALLS

With A, ch 14.

Row 1 (RS): Hdc in 4th ch from hook (ch lp created here counts as first hdc), hdc in each ch across, turn—12 hdc.

Row 2: Ch 2 (counts as hdc here and throughout), hdc in each of next 10 sts, hdc in top of turning ch, turn—12 hdc.

Row 3: Ch 2, hdc in each of next 3 sts, turn, leaving rem sts unworked—4 hdc.

Row 4: Ch 2, hdc in each of next 2 sts, hdc in top of ch-2 turning ch, turn—4 hdc.

Row 5: Ch 2, hdc in each of next 2 sts, hdc in top of ch-2 turning ch, ch 10—4 hdc, 10 ch.

Row 6: Hdc in 4th ch from hook, hdc in each of next 6 ch, hdc in each of next 3 hdc, hdc in top of ch-2 turning ch, turn—12 hdc.

Row 7: Ch 2, hdc in each of next 10 sts, hdc in top of ch-2 turning ch, turn—12 hdc.

Row 8: Ch 2, FPhdc around each of next 10 sts, FPhdc around ch-2 turning ch, turn—12 sts. This row creates a ridge on RS of piece to represent corner of house.

Row 9: Ch 3 (counts as dc here and throughout), dc in each of next 3 sts, ch 2, sk next 2 sts, dc in next st, ch 2, sk next 2 sts, dc in each of next 2 sts, dc in top of ch-2 turning ch, turn—8 dc, 2 ch-2 sps.

Row 10: Ch 3, dc in each of next 2 sts, ch 2, sk next ch-2 sp, dc in next dc, ch 2, sk next ch-2 sp, dc in each of next 3 sts, dc in top of ch-3 turning ch, turn—8 dc, 2 ch-2 sps.

Row 11: Ch 2, hdc in each of next 10 sts, hdc in top of ch-3 turning ch, turn—12 hdc.

Row 12: Ch 3, dc in each of next 2 sts, ch 2, sk next 2 dc, dc in next dc, ch 2, sk next 2 dc, dc in each of next 3 sts, dc in top of ch-2 turning ch, turn—8 dc, 2 ch-2 sps.

Row 13: Ch 3, dc in each of next 3 sts, ch 2, sk next ch-2 sp, dc in next st, ch 2, sk next ch-2 sp, dc in each of next 2 sts, dc in top of ch-3 turning ch, turn—8 dc, 2 ch-2 sp.

Row 14: Ch 2, hdc in each of next 10 sts, hdc in top of ch-3 turning ch, turn—12 hdc.

Row 15: Ch 1, sl st in first st, sl st in each of next 10 sts, sl st in top of ch-2 turning ch.

Outline Row: Ch 1, rotate piece to work along bottom edge of house, working in row-end sts, work 12 sl sts evenly-spaced across to corner ridge (made in row 8), work 3 sl sts across to door opening corner, ch 4, sk door opening, sl st in next corner at top of row 2, work 3 sl st evenly spaced across to corner of house with last st in first ch st of foundation ch of house;

Rotate piece to work up side of house, ch 1, working in opposite side of foundation ch, sl st in first ch (already holding a sl st), sl st in next 10 ch, sl st in first ch of turning ch at end of row;

Rotate piece to work across top of house, ch 1 and PM in this st, work 11 sl sts evenly-spaced across door section to corner ridge, work 13 sl sts evenly spaced across window section to far corner. Fasten off A.

GABLE END

For a fancier edge, see Picot Trim Gable End in "Features," page 136.

Row 1: Working in BLO, with a slip knot of A on hook, yo, draw up lp in st with marker, yo, draw up lp in next sl st, yo, draw through all lps on hook (hdc2tog, dec complete), hdc in each of next 7 sts, hdc2tog over next 2 sts, turn—9 sts.

Row 2: Ch 3, sk first hdc, hdc2tog over next 2 sts, hdc in each of next 4 sts, hdc2tog over last 2 sts, turn—7 sts.

Row 3: Ch 3, sk first hdc, hdc2tog over next 2 sts, hdc in each of next 2 sts, hdc2tog over next st and top of ch-3 turning ch, turn—5 sts.

Row 4: Ch 3, sk first hdc, hdc2tog over next 2 sts, hdc2tog over next st and top of ch-3 turning ch, turn—3 sts.

Row 5: Ch 1, sc3tog over first 3 sts. Fasten off A.

Side outline: Draw up a lp of A in st with marker, work 9 sl sts evenly spaced up slanted edge of gable, ending with a sl st in top of row 5. Fasten off A. Weave in ends, lightly tacking turning chs to decreases in order to close gaps.

ROOF

With B, ch 16.

Row 1 (RS): Continuing along BLO of sl sts at top of house, yo, insert hook in 4th ch from hook and in next sl st of house top, draw up lp, yo and draw through all lps on hook (first hdc complete), using the same method, hdc in each of next 10 sts of ch and in corresponding sts on top of house, hdc2tog over last 2 ch and corresponding sl st on top of house, turn—13 sts (counting turning ch as st).

Row 2: Working into sts of roof only, ch 3 (counts as dc), sk first hdc, hdc2tog over next 2 sts, hdc in each of next 9 sts, 2 hdc in top of ch-3 turning ch, turn—13 sts.

Row 3: Ch 3, hdc in first st, hdc in each of next 10 sts, hdc2tog over next st and top of ch-3 turning ch, turn—13 sts.

Row 4: Rep Row 2.

Row 5: Ch 5, sl st in 2nd ch from hook (for picot), sk next 3 ch (counts as dc), hdc in first st in row 4, hdc in each of next 10 sts, hdc2tog over next st and top of ch-3 turning ch—13 sts, 1 picot. Fasten off B. Weave in ends, gently tacking turning chs to decreases (rows 2 and 4) to close gaps.

Roof edge: Draw up a lp of B in st with marker, remove marker, ch 1, sc in same st, sl st in BLO of each of next 9 sl sts, sl st in picot at tip of main roof piece. Leaving long sewing length, fasten off B. Use sewing length to sew together the abutting edges of gable and roof. Weave in ends.

DOOR

Working in the opposite side of foundation ch at base of row 6.

Door Row 1: Join C with sc in first ch of ch-3 turning ch at base of row 6, sc in each of next 7 ch, turn—8 sc.

Door Row 2: Ch 2, hdc in next st, ch 2, sk next 2 sts, hdc in each of next 4 sts, turn—6 hdc, ch-2 sp.

Door Row 3: Ch 1, sc in first hdc, sc in each of next 7 sts—8 sc. Fasten off C. Weave in ends.

FEATURES

Picot Trim Gable End

With A or desired gable end color, [slst-picot, ch 1] 5 times, slst-picot once more, turn.

Counting each ch-1 and the base of each picot as one stitch, you have 11 sts to work into, which exactly matches the number of sl-sts at the top of the door section of the house.

Ch 1, insert hook into base of first picot and into BL of first sl st on top of door section of house, pull up lp, ch 3. Continue to work, inserting hook into next st of picot trim and into BL of next sl st, working through double thickness, hdc2tog over next 2 sts, hdc in each of next 6 sts, hdc2tog over next 2 sts, turn. Finish gable end as above, Rows 2-5.

Lintels

(they hold up the wall above window and door openings; not to be confused with lentils, which are legumes): Make a line of tambour st (see page 11) immediately above door or window openings, beginning about 1 st before the opening and ending about 1 st after the opening.

Lintel Alternatives

Embroider lintels or crochet heavier lintels (like one row of sc).

Gable Vent

Ch 4, join with sl st in first ch to form ring, ch 1, 6 sc in ring, leaving long end for sewing, cut yarn and needle join to first st of rnd. Sew to gable end, close to peak.

Chimney

With RS facing, join A with hdc in 7th roof st from gable peak, hdc in each of next 2 sts. Fasten off A.

Window Box

Ch 5, sc in 2nd ch from hook, sc in each ch across. Fasten off, leaving a long sewing length. Fasten off. Sew under windows, embroider flowers or use beads to represent flowers.

Shrubbery

Crochet a few circles of varying sizes as below, use photo as inspiration for arranging them, sew in place. Save time by leaving long ends for sewing when you cut yarn.

Small circle

Same as gable vent.

Hdc circle: Ch 4, join with a sl st in first ch to form a ring, ch 2, 11 hdc in ring, cut thread and needle-join to first st of rnd.

Dc circle: Ch 4, join with sl st in first ch to form ring, ch 3, 14 dc in ring, cut yarn and needle-join in first st of rnd.

FINISHING

Block pieces, weave in any rem ends.

Add more features as desired. Think of new features, like a row of picots across the top of the roof, a path leading from the door, smoke coming from the chimney.

mamas and papas

No family is complete without parental units. You'll have plenty of options with these motifs to crochet the parent or parents that best match your family—even if your family is out of this world!

SKILL LEVEL
Intermediate

MATERIALS & TOOLS
5 or more colors of yarn as desired: Skin (A), hair (B), dress or shirt (C), pants (D), shoes (E)

Crochet hook: Appropriate size hook to achieve a firm gauge with selected yarn

Tapestry needle

Optional: Embroidery floss, beads, or buttons for embellishment, with sewing needle and thread

PATTERN NOTES
Feel free to customize this pattern! You'll find a selection of hairdos here, but you can style the hair any way you want. Arms can be positioned in various ways, and you may need to crochet an arm more than once before you find the perfect arrangement. Luckily, the pieces are small. Adjust the height of people by adding rows or sts, or taking them away. Alter their clothing. Have fun!

Instructions for tambour st are on page 11.

ABBREVIATIONS
Find instructions on pages 16 and 17 for: BL, dc2tog, hdc2tog, htr, htr2tog, joined-dc, joined-tr, RS, sc2tog, sc3tog, slst-picot, WS

home

FOR THESE PEOPLE WE USED

Classic Elite Yarns Liberty Wool (100% washable wool; 1¾oz/50g = 122yd/111m) DK/sport weight yarn (3): #7801 Bleach (A), #7880 Golden Poppy (B), #7858 Scarlet (C), #7857 Bright Blue (D), #7813 Ebony (E).

GAUGE CIRCLE
(see page 7) = ⅞"/2.2cm worked on 4.00mm (size G-6 U.S.) hook

FINISHED MEASUREMENT
5⅝"/14.3cm to 6"/15.2cm tall from top of head (excluding hair)

Cascade 220 Sport (100% Peruvian Highland wool; 1.75oz/50g = 164yd/15m) light weight yarn (3): #8622 Camel or #8686 Brown (A), #8686 Brown or #8555 Black (B), #7802 Cerise or #7827 Goldenrod or #2409 Palm or #7825 Orange Sherbet (C), #9568 Twilight Blue or #2409 Palm (D), #9568 Twilight Blue or #8555 Black or #7825 Orange Sherbet or #8622 Camel (E).

GAUGE CIRCLE
(see page 7) = ⅞"/2.2cm worked on 3.50mm (size E-4 U.S.) hook

FINISHED MEASUREMENT
5½"/14cm to 5¾"/14.6cm tall from top of head (excluding hair)

Berroco Ultra® Alpaca Light (50% super fine alpaca, 50% Peruvian wool; 1.75oz/50g = 144yd/133m) sport weight yarn (2): #4275 Pea Soup Mix (A), #4234 Cardinal (B), #4217 Tupelo (C), #42191 Azure Mix (D), #4280 Mahogany Mix (E).

GAUGE CIRCLE
(see page 7) = ⅞"/2.2cm worked on 3.75mm (size F-5 U.S.) hook

FINISHED MEASUREMENT
5⅝"/14.3cm to 6"/15.2cm tall from top of head (excluding hair and antennae)

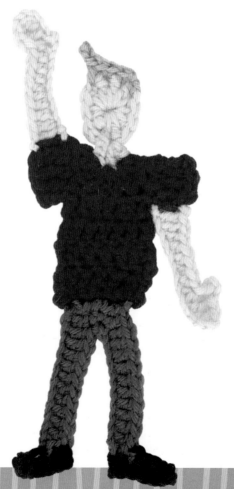

INSTRUCTIONS

MAMA
With A, ch 5, join with sl st to first ch to form a ring.

Face (RS)
Ch 3 (counts as dc), (2 htr, dc, 2 hdc, dc, 2 htr, dc, 2 hdc) in ring, join with sl st to top of beg ch-3—12 sts.

Neck
Sl st in next st, (sl st, ch 3, 2 dc) in next st—3 dc. Fasten off A.

Choose a hairstyle from the "Hairstyles" sidebar and crochet it with color B.

Mama's Dress
Row 1: Looking at WS of neck, join C with 4 dc in first dc of neck, 2 dc in next st, 4 dc in top of ch-3 at end of neck, turn—10 dc.

Row 2 (RS): Ch 4, make a 4tr-cluster as follows: *(yo twice, draw up a lp, yo, draw through 2 lps, yo, draw through 2 lps) twice* in the first dc; rep from * to * in the 2nd dc; after repeating you should have 5 lps on hook—yo, draw through all lps on hook, ch 4, sl st in 2nd dc (first sleeve made);

Continuing in same direction, ch 3, dc in each of next 2 sts, dc2tog over next 2 sts, dc in each of next 2 sts, ch 3, sl st in next st (body sts made);

Ch 4, make a 4tr-cluster as above with the first 2 sts in the same st as last sl st, and next 2 sts in the last st of the row, ch 4, sl st in last st of row (2nd sleeve made), turn—2 sleeves made with tr-clusters and 5 dc for waist. Fasten off C.

Waist and Skirt

Row 3 (worked in the 5 dc between the tr-cluster sleeves): With WS facing, sk ch-3 at edge of waist, rejoin C with dc in first dc of waist, dc in each of next 4 dc, turn—5 dc.

Row 4 (RS): Ch 3 (counts as dc here and throughout), dc in first st, dc in each of next 3 sts, 2 dc in last st, turn—7 sts.

Row 5: Ch 3, dc in first st, dc in each of next 5 sts, 2 dc in top of turning ch, turn—9 sts.

Row 6: Ch 3, dc in first st, dc in each of next 7 sts, 2 dc in top of turning ch, turn—11 sts.

Row 7: Ch 3, joined-dc in next st, dc in each of next 8 sts, dc in top of turning ch, turn—11 sts.

Row 8: Rep Row 7, do not turn. Fasten off C.

Mama's Legs, Feet, and Shoes

LEG 1 (RS)
Sk first 3 sts of Row 8, join A with sl st in BL of next st, ch 11, sc in 2nd ch from hook, sc in each of next 2 ch, 3 sc in next ch (for

heel), sc in each of next 2 ch, hdc in each of next 4 ch, join with sl st to next st of Row 8. Fasten off A.

SHOE 1
With RS facing, join E with sl st in the turning ch at the tip of the toe, working along the bottom of the foot, 2 sc in first sc, sc in each of next 3 sts, (sc, sl st) in next sc. Fasten off E.

LEG 2 (RS)
Sk next st of Row 8, join A with sl st in BL of next st, ch 13, sc in 2nd ch from hook, sc in each of next 2 ch, sc3tog over next 3 ch-sts (for heel), sc in each of next 2 ch, hdc in each of next 4 ch, join with sl st to next st of Row 8. Fasten off A.

SHOE 2
With RS facing, join E with (sl st, sc) in the free lp of the ch at the center of the heel, working across the opposite side of

foundation ch on bottom of the foot, sc in each of next 3 ch, 2 sc in next ch, rotate foot to work in the top of the foot, sl st in the first sc of foot. Fasten off E.

Mama's Arms
(require 2 sts of sleeve)
Read "Arms" sidebar on page 00.

THUMB-FIRST ARM
Join A with sl st in BL of a sleeve st, ch 7, slst-picot for thumb, ch 4. Working back along chain, hdc in 3rd ch from hook, hdc in next ch, sc in base of thumb, sc in each of next 3 ch, [for bent arm, work 2 hdc in next ch; for straight arm, work hdc in next ch], hdc in each of last 3 ch, join with sl st in BL of next sleeve st. Fasten off.

HAND-FIRST ARM
Join A with sl st in BL of a sleeve st, ch 13 for bent arm or 12 for straight arm, hdc in 3rd ch from hook, hdc in next ch, slst-

HAIRSTYLES

Crochet as written with hair color (B), or study these and then create your own crocheted hairstyle.

Flip

Looking at RS of face/neck piece, sk 1 st after last st of neck, join B with sl st in next st, ch 6, draw up a lp in 2nd, 3rd, and 4th ch from hook, yo and draw through all lps on hook (sc3tog made), hdc in next st, 2 hdc in each of next 5 sts, hdc in next st, ch 2, sl st in next st, ch 4, turn, draw up a lp in 2nd, 3rd, and 4th ch from hook, yo and draw through all lps on hook (sc3tog made), turn and sl st in first available hdc—2 flips plus 13 hdc and ch-2. Fasten off B.

Long Hair

Ch 10, sc in 3rd ch from hook, sc in each ch across; looking at RS of face/neck piece, sk 1 st after last st of neck, hdc in each of next 2 sts, 2 hdc in each of next 5 sts, hdc in each of next 2 sts, ch 10, sc in 3rd ch from hook, sc in each ch across, sl st to same st at base of last hdc, fasten off B OR for better results, cut yarn and needle-join in same st as last hdc.

Cleopatra Hair

Looking at RS of face/neck piece, sk 1 st after last st of neck, join B with tr in next st, 2 htr in next st, (dc, hdc) in next st, 2 hdc in each of next 3 sts, (hdc, dc) in next st, 2 htr in next st, tr in next st—16 sts. Fasten off B.

Crew Cut

Looking at RS of face/neck piece, sk 3 sts after last st of neck, join B with hdc in next st, sc in next 2 sts, hdc in next st—4 sts. Fasten off.

Tin Tin Hair

Looking at RS of face/neck piece, sk 3 sts after last st of neck, join B with hdc in next st, sc in next 2 sts, hdc in next st, ch 2—4 sts and ch-2. Fasten off.

Antennae

Looking at RS of face/neck piece, sk 4 sts after last st of neck, join A or desired color in FL of next st, *ch 8, (2 hdc, ch 2, sl st) in 3rd ch from hook, sl st in each of next 5 ch, sl st in FL of same st of head*, sl st in FL of next st; rep from * to * once. Note: Working in FL allows you to add a hairstyle behind the antennae—make the hairstyle as instructed, only work in the BL of the sts with the antennae in them.

Martian Sweep

Looking at RS of face/neck piece, sk 1 st after last st of neck, join B with sc in next st, hdc in next st, 2 hdc in next st, (hdc, dc) in next st, (dc, htr) in next st, 3 tr in next st, 2 tr in each of next 2 sts, PM in last st of head with a tr in it, ch 15, sl st in 2nd ch from hook, sc in next ch, sc2tog over next 2 ch, hdc in next ch, hdc2tog over next 2 ch, dc in next ch, dc2tog over next 2 ch, htr in next ch, htr2tog over next 2 ch, 2 tr in next ch, join with sl st to marked st, remove marker. Fasten off.

Martian Spike

Looking at RS of face/neck piece, sk 2 sts after last st of neck, join B with sl st in next st, *ch 4, hdc in 2nd ch from hook, sl st in next 2 ch-sts, sl st in next st of head; rep from * 4 or 5 times. Fasten off.

picot for thumb, sc2tog over next 2 ch, sc in next 2 ch, [for bent arm, work hdc2tog over next 2 ch; for straight arm, work hdc in next ch], hdc in last 3 ch, join with sl st in BL of next sleeve st. Fasten off.

PAPA

Make Papa's head and neck as for Mama's head and neck, above. Add a hairstyle from the "Hairstyle" sidebar.

Papa's Shirt

Row 1: Looking at WS of neck, join C with 3 htr in first dc of neck, 3 dc in next st, 3 htr in top of ch-3 turning chain of neck, turn—9 sts.

Row 2 (RS): Ch 4 (counts as tr), joined-tr in first st, tr in next st, (tr, ch 2, sl st in side of tr, ch 1, sl st) in next st (first sleeve made), ch 3, 2 dc in next st, dc in next st, 2 dc in next st, ch 3 (body sts made), (sl st, ch 4, joined-tr) in next st, tr in next st, (tr, ch 2, sl st in side of tr, ch 1, sl st) in next st (second sleeve made), turn. Fasten off C.

Row 3 (WS): With WS facing, rejoin C with dc in top of ch-3 at beg of Row 2 of body sts, dc in each of next 5 dc, dc in top of ch-3 turning ch, turn—7 dc.

Row 4: Ch 3 (counts as dc here and throughout), joined-dc in next st, dc in each of next 5 dc, turn—7 dc.

Row 5: Ch 3, joined-dc in next st, dc in each of next 4 dc, dc in top of ch-3 turning ch—7 dc. Fasten off C.

Papa's Trousers and Shoes

Row 1 (RS): With RS facing, sk first st of Shirt Row 5, join D with sl st in BL of next st, ch 16, dc in 5th ch from hook (this creates a ch-4 lp at the end of the leg), dc

This is to supplement the st-by-st instructions provided. In general, join an arm with sl st in the edge of a sleeve, ch, and then work back toward sleeve using sts that form a hand, thumb, and arm.

Study the arms in the pictures. Find where each arm joins the sleeve and how the sts come back and rejoin the sleeve. As you follow the ch out toward the hand, notice how sometimes the thumb is formed first, while other times the hand is formed first. Figure out how "thumb-first" and "hand-first" arms work for holding hands, waving, or gesturing.

For example, the Mama in the red dress waves with her "hand-first" right arm; her left arm is "thumb-first." Both arms of the Papa in the yellow shirt are "hand-first."

Decide how you want each arm of your crocheted Mama or Papa to look. Visualize whether thumb or hand will be first, then follow instructions for "thumb-first" or "hand-first" arm. Make the arms. Are they what you wanted? If yes, good! If not, try again.

in each of next 11 sts, sk 1 st of Shirt Row 5, sl st in BL of next st, ch 1, turn—12 dc plus turning ch.

Row 2: Sc in each of next 2 sts, ch 14, turn.

Row 3: Dc in 5th ch from hook (this creates a ch-4 lp at the end of the leg), dc in each of next 9 ch, dc in each of next 2 sc, sk 1 st of Shirt Row 5, sl st in BL of next st. Fasten off D, leaving a sewing length. Use sewing length to tack dc sts at top of trousers to lower edge of shirt.

SHOE 1

With RS facing, join E with sl st on the outside of the first trouser leg, in the first ch of the ch-4 lp, ch 5, sc in 2nd ch from hook, hdc in each of next 3 ch, hdc in each of next 2 ch of ch-4 lp of trouser leg. Fasten off E.

SHOE 2

Beginning at the inside of the 2nd trouser leg, join E with hdc in the 2nd ch of the ch-4 lp, hdc in next ch-st, ch 5, turn, sc in 2nd ch from hook, hdc in each of next 3 ch, sl st to last ch of ch-4 lp of leg. Fasten off E.

Papa's Arms
(require 3 sts of sleeve)

Read the "Arms" sidebar at right.

THUMB-FIRST ARM

With RS facing, join A with sl st in BL of a sleeve st, ch 8, slst-picot for thumb, ch 5; working back along chain, dc in 4th ch from hook, dc in next ch, hdc in base of thumb, hdc in each of next 3 ch, [for bent arm, work 2 hdc in next ch; for straight arm, work hdc in next ch], hdc in each of next 2 ch, dc in each of last 2 ch, sk 1 sleeve st, join with sl st in BL of next sleeve st. Fasten off A.

HAND-FIRST ARM

With RS facing, join A with sl st in BL of a sleeve st, ch 15 for bent arm or 14 for straight arm, dc in 4th ch from hook, dc in next ch, slst-picot for thumb, hdc2tog over next 2 ch, hdc in each of next 2 ch, [for bent arm, work hdc2tog over next 2 ch; for straight arm, work hdc in next ch], hdc in each of next 2 ch, dc in each of last 2 ch, sk 1 sleeve st, join with sl st in BL of next sleeve st. Fasten off A.

FINISHING

Weave in ends. Block pieces. Embellish with embroidery, sl-st outlines, beads, or tiny buttons if desired.

OUR FAVORITE MARTIANS

Families come in all forms—even extra-terrestrial! After a long day heading up top-secret intergalactic missions, Rog and Pam come home to down-to-earth chores, like making sure the kids eat their jellied gree-worm and signing mid-term report cards from Andromeda Prep School.

ACKNOWLEDGMENTS

Thank You, talented and patient folks at Lark Crafts—Shannon Quinn-Tucker, Amanda Carestio, Karen Manthey, Karen Levy, Steve Mann, and Shannon Yokeley. I'm so glad to be on your team!

Thank You, dear family!—Charles, for taking up my slack and for being a willing partner in all our undertakings; Eva and Ella, for saying, "Aww, Mom! That's so cuuuuuuute!" whenever necessary; Mom and Dad, for being proud of me—I try each and every day to live up to that honor.

Thank You, Dublin Rippers—Donna, Hazel, Mindy, Peggy, Rachel, and Sonja! You've been with me through this whole book, freely giving encouragement, laughter, and companionship. I look forward to our Tuesday mornings together.

And finally, Thank You…

Yarn Suppliers!

Berroco
www.berroco.com

Cascade Yarns
www.cascadeyarns.com

Classic Elite Yarns
www.classiceliteyarns.com

Coats & Clark
www.coatsandclark.com

Dale of Norway
daleofnorway-1.shptron.com

Lion Brand Yarn
www.lionbrand.com

Plymouth Yarn
www.plymouthyarn.com

ABOUT THE AUTHOR

When I was a child, my family took roadtrips through Texas. We went to reunions, funerals, or to visit aunts and uncles or friends. We drove through many a small town, where I saw the words "WOOL & MOHAIR" boldly painted on warehouses and feed stores. I imagined shelves piled high with colorful, cuddly, fantastic yarns just waiting for someone like me to crochet or knit them. Since we never stopped to look inside the warehouses, my lovely daydream continued until, as an adult, I knew better.

Even at a tender age, I was clearly a confirmed crocheter and knitter. Later, I made items for sale, but mass production and selling were not my idea of a fun career. In the early 1990s, I learned how to go about publishing my original designs. This was the perfect fit for me: a great deal of solitary work, mixed with exactly the right amount of teamwork with editors, and a smattering of teaching thrown in for variety. My design career has allowed me to be true to my nature.

My husband and I have two daughters, one in college and one at home for a few more years. For the last ten years we have been planning and building an earthen house. That project is drawing to a close as this book goes to press. And I eventually got to see the inside of a Wool & Mohair warehouse. It wasn't anything like I imagined, but it was wonderful the way it was.

Read about Suzann's visit to a Western Wool & Mohair warehouse here: *www.textilefusion.com/blog/?p=217*

See more photos of W&M warehouses here: *www.textilefusion.com/blog/?p=219*

See more of Suzann's work in her previous books: *Crochet Bouquet* (Lark, 2008) and *Crochet Garden* (Lark, 2012).

Elementary School Star Template

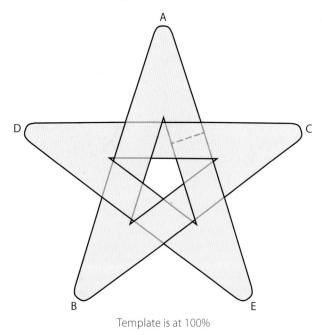

Template is at 100%

Editors: Shannon Quinn-Tucker and Amanda Carestio

Art Director: Shannon Yokeley

Photographer: Steve Mann

Illustrator: Lauren J. Patton

Cover Designer: Shannon Yokeley